LEADING FOR SCHOOL LIBRARIANS

ALA Neal-Schuman purchases fund advocacy, awareness, and accreditation programs for library professionals worldwide.

LEADING

for SCHOOL LIBRARIANS

There Is No Other Option   HILDA K. WEISBURG

Foreword by Susan D. Ballard

An imprint of the American Library Association

CHICAGO   2017

HILDA K. WEISBURG was a school librarian for over 30 years and is now an author, speaker, and adjunct instructor at William Paterson University (NJ). She coauthored fourteen books for school librarians (with Ruth Toor), including two for ALA Editions, *Being Indispensable: A School Librarian's Guide to Becoming an Invaluable Leader* (2011), *New on the Job: A School Library Media Specialist's Guide to Success* (2007) and *School Librarian's Career Planner* (2013), which was her first work without Ruth who has fully retired. Hilda has since done a 2nd edition of *New on the Job* which has been an ALA best seller since its 2007 publication. For 35 years she cowrote and edited *School Librarian's Workshop*, a bimonthly newsletter for K–12 librarians. She has given presentations at ALA, AASL, and state library conferences and given staff development workshops in many locations. A past president of the New Jersey Association of School Librarians, she is a past chair of AASL Advocacy, Chairs The Ruth Toor Grant for Strong Public Libraries, and serves on the ALA Professional Ethics Committee. Her YA fantasy novel, *Woven through Time* was a finalist in the International Book Award in the Fiction/ Fantasy category and has received ten 5-star reviews on Amazon. She is now working on the sequel.

© 2017 by Hilda K. Weisburg

Extensive effort has gone into ensuring the reliability of the information in this book; however, the publisher makes no warranty, express or implied, with respect to the material contained herein.

ISBN: 978-0-8389-1510-3 (paper)

Library of Congress Cataloging-in-Publication Data
Names: Weisburg, Hilda K., 1942- author.
Title: Leading for school librarians : there is no other option / Hilda K. Weisburg.
Description: Chicago : Neal-Schuman, an imprint of the American Library Association, 2017. | Includes bibliographical references and index.
Identifiers: LCCN 2016047254 | ISBN 9780838915103 (pbk. : alk. paper)
Subjects: LCSH: School librarians—Psychology. | School librarians—Professional relationships. | School libraries—United States—Administration. | Leadership.
Classification: LCC Z682.4.S34 W45 2017 | DDC 027.8—dc23 LC record available at https://lccn.loc.gov/2016047254

Cover design by Kim Thornton. Images: © double A/Shutterstock, Inc. (top);
© Rawpixel.com/Shutterstock, Inc. (bottom).
Text design by Alejandra Diaz in the Expo Serif Pro and VistaSans typefaces.

♾ This paper meets the requirements of ANSI/NISO Z39.48–1992 (Permanence of Paper).

Printed in the United States of America
21 20 19 18 17   5 4 3 2 1

To the School Library Leaders—past, present, and future:

To past leaders who were my role models and mentors, with my unending gratitude.

To current leaders who are my friends and colleagues, with admiration and love.

To future leaders who are emerging or considering taking the first steps, with the hope that this book will speed your journey.

Together we transform learning, our communities, and the world.

CONTENTS

FOREWORD

Leadership—one word, yet endless impact. While there are many forms of leadership, as well as numerous variations on the theme of how to go about finding one's own leadership style and learning what will work for us in the landscape and organizational culture in which we operate, Hilda Weisburg wants to make sure we understand one thing from the very beginning: *Every* librarian is a leader, and that means you, too. As she succinctly states up front in Chapter 1, ". . . leadership is not an option—it is a job responsibility."

Leading for School Librarians is part history lesson, part master class, part cautionary tale, and always spot on in providing information and strategies that will illuminate the sometimes scary pathway to finding our own inner leader. Hilda shares her expertise and, yes, her opinions, too. But those opinions are educated, firmly grounded in experience, and the result of a lifetime spent in the pursuit of continuous improvement of program and practice. They count for something—in fact, they count for a lot! Throughout the many years I have known and admired Hilda, I have never, not once, seen her shirk a task or a responsibility. In fact, she steps up with tenacity and verve, even though she readily admits throughout this book that she hasn't always seen herself as a leader.

As school librarians, we can identify with this acknowledgment, as all too often we don't see ourselves as leaders, because we view our organizations as hierarchies in which we have low visibility and/or are marginalized. Don't expect a pass from Hilda on that account. Empathy yes, but she'll make you realize there is no excuse for not getting in the game. Early in her career she also had fears, doubts, obstacles, barriers, and the criticism of naysayers. So, how did she manage to take her first leap toward leadership? She stuck her neck out and by networking, getting involved, asking for help, and sharing her own story, as well as listening to and learning from others, a leader emerged. With deep understanding, she now challenges us to never stop reimagining the role and relevance of the school librarian to positively impact student achievement and to recognize our role as catalysts for teaching and learning in the contemporary educational environment. In this book, she is reaching out to provide the same sort of assistance and guidance she has received along the way.

I love the fact that Hilda acknowledges those monsters in the closet and under the bed which keep us up at night, such as the effect of external factors we can't always control but to which we need to respond (education reform initiatives, standardized testing, politics, etc.), as well as internal factors (school culture, stakeholder needs) that shape the daily context in the preK–12 ecosystem. Yet, again, she won't allow us to use them as an excuse to stand on the sidelines. She promotes our understanding of, but not our dwelling on, the current and emerging learning environmental influences and how this understanding can help us to overcome barriers, even if they seem insurmountable. Hilda consistently reminds us that, despite the unrelenting impact of these factors, we must stay focused on alignment of the mission and vision of the school library program to that of the school, in order to maintain a steady course and maneuver around any obstacles.

The way the book is structured lends itself to the development of our own individualized personal plans for leadership. We get the lay of the land in Part I and gain a context for what on-the-ground school librarianship looks like, as well as learn about the characteristics of a leader and how we can begin to develop seedling strategies to cultivate these dispositions in ourselves. In particular, I found myself nodding in agreement at Hilda's discussion of "imposter syndrome" (Chapter 5): those moments of self-doubt that creep up on you, distract your focus, and if not held in check, minimize your effectiveness. None of us is expert in everything, Hilda admonishes. This put me in mind of Voltaire's observation, "Don't let the perfect be the enemy of the good." Hilda and Voltaire—on the same wavelength, *naturellement!*

Part II provides next steps to ramp up our impact and build influence and relationships. We are exposed to solid theory about types of power and which ones we should seek to optimize, as well as how to inventory and leverage our strengths and personal skill sets. Additionally, there is focus on how to grow our leadership expertise *vis-à-vis* time and priorities management and to build capacity in various areas of communication. In this section, Hilda wants us to be cognizant of the potential to become complacent if we see ourselves as "good" practitioners and don't constantly strive to become "great" at what we do. Again, no need to be perfect, but there is a need to be great and always striving! I don't think it a fluke that throughout the book, and in particular here, Hilda models the conversational, yet respectful and professional tone she wants us to emulate in our relationships and communications with others because she knows it works.

In Part III, there is the opportunity to add things up and stretch our mindset, as Hilda introduces us to concepts that are standard operating procedure in the business world and which we need to modify and adapt to help serve, advocate for, and express the needs and the value-added aspects of our programs. Strategic planning, goal setting, establishing and delivering on our brand identity, and risk and gap analysis techniques are all brought into mix. In her discussions about empowering stakeholders, Hilda shows school librarian leadership as a collaborative, flexible process that blends the agency of various types of expertise within the learning community. It occurs when all those responsible for student learning accept leadership in their particular area of focus. It is also a social process through shared and active engagement to address situations and issues, and involves a commitment to reflective practice and continuous improvement.

As Part III concludes, Hilda evokes one of my very favorite words—"joy." You will experience pure unadulterated joy if you heed her advice and pay it forward through involvement in state and national professional associations, through sharing expertise by writing and presenting about what you know and have learned in order to advance and improve our profession and education, and by living a balanced life in which you can set aside (though likely never forget) your passion for school librarianship when family, friends, and adventure call you! Don't apologize or feel guilty for en"joy"ing your life.

I am also struck by the "Key Ideas" at the end of each chapter which is a bulleted list that can serve as a daily mantra. By my count, there are 317 Key Ideas—many of which bear repeating so that they add up to equal 365. Think about it—daily notions to reflect on and internalize throughout the year. The intellectual exercise is enlightening, to say the least, and helping to engrain these critical ideas into our professional consciousness.

Is it any wonder Hilda Weisburg is a recipient of AASL's most prestigious award for individual contribution to our profession? This "Distinguished Service Award" honoree now honors us by sharing her vision for our future, which involves planning to reimagine roles and responsibilities and how to best leverage programs, expertise, and resources, to ensure students and teachers engage and participate more fully in the new learning landscape. Hilda's message is for each of us to recognize the need to be future-ready, embrace our respective roles as leaders, and help move our learning communities forward. In the words of my fellow Granite Stater Daniel Webster, "There is always room at the top." You are needed there because the future is now and we must all be part of it. Hilda expects no less, and we cannot disappoint her.

Onward!

Susan D. Ballard

INTRODUCTION

Over the years, the library profession has evolved in ways beyond the awareness of most non-educators and many who are in the field. Technology is an obvious area. But another equally important one is the reaction to the wholesale loss of jobs and even libraries as a result of the economic collapse in 2008.

School librarians were the hardest hit as boards of education and administrators scrambled to cope with severe budget cuts. Working alone and believing that schools would always need and want librarians, they were totally unprepared for the calamity that ensued. Determined to forestall future decimations of programs, many library schools incorporated advocacy into their curriculum, recognizing that those in all types of libraries need to know how to develop supporters for their programs.

Burdened by a heavier workload (also a result of economic conditions) and the constant need to keep abreast of changing technology and government standards and requirements, school librarians have struggled with how to advocate for their program. It seems to many that advocacy is about begging to keep your job rather than recognizing that advocacy is becoming so indispensable to stakeholders, they fight to keep you.

The problem is that talking about advocacy is putting the cart before the horse. You can't be an advocate if you aren't a leader. Interestingly enough, library school courses don't often address leadership, and for many, school librarians are intimidated by the thought of becoming a leader.

As stated in the subtitle of this book, the truth in today's climate is that "There is no other option." Librarians must learn how to lead in order for their programs to succeed and thrive. In other types of libraries, there is a way to advance. Librarians work with those who are further up the hierarchy and see what library leadership looks like. While not perfect, they have living models. And they aren't alone.

The preponderance of school librarians are alone in their buildings. They have no models of library leadership. They have their workload and their fears.

Yet, their ultimate survival rests on their ability to be recognized as a leader in their building.

I have spent much of my career working to help librarians be their best and promote the value of their programs. For many years now, I have been writing, blogging, and presenting workshops on leadership. But I still meet so many librarians who don't know how to get started and don't believe they have what it takes to be a leader.

They look at national or even state leaders and think they never could do that. I realized they were looking at the finished product and didn't see that many small steps preceded becoming a state association president or other recognized leader. Strongly believing that anyone who wants to become a leader can do it, I embarked on this project.

I hope you find truth in the Lao Tzu quote, "A journey of a thousand miles begins with one small step," and begin your own journey with Chapter 1. If you gradually implement what is discussed and recommended, by the time you have completed the final chapter you will have embraced your ability to lead and will be seen as vital and indispensable. You will be a leader and have many advocates for your program.

Hilda K. Weisburg

PART I

SAFE FIRST STEPS TO LEADERSHIP

School librarians have the best job in the world. They make their libraries a welcoming environment, promote twenty-first century learning, integrate the latest educational websites and apps into their teaching, and connect students to the perfect book, to build a love of reading. Through the library program, students become lifelong learners, as well as successful members and contributors in a participatory society that spans the globe.

Encompassing all that into one program would be an exhausting task in and of itself, but the realities of today's school culture exponentially increase the daily difficulties and stresses. If you are an elementary librarian, you are probably chained to a fixed schedule with one class following hard on the heels of another. Many find they have little or no opportunity to meet with teachers. If you are a middle- or high-school librarian, you might have a flexible schedule but must work diligently to get past teacher resistance to bringing their classes to the library, while feeling the pressure of meeting the demands of state-imposed standards tied to testing and often your own evaluation.

At all levels, budgets have been slashed, leaving little money for new acquisitions and causing collections to be woefully outdated. Clerks who once were common at the secondary level have been eliminated in many places. Staffing has been cut, forcing many librarians to either serve multiple schools or leaving a single librarian in a school with 2,000 students. Technology (other than computers for testing) is hard to come by. Bandwidth limits the number of devices that can be used.

But listing what is wrong serves no one. This is the new reality, and you must learn to not only live with it but thrive within it. The question is, "How do you manage to be successful in this environment?" The answer is, somehow, you must become a leader.

For years, the American Association of School Librarians (AASL) has been exhorting librarians to become leaders in their buildings and districts. Many have done so, but most librarians are still working hard at their day-to-day tasks, unable to see beyond them. The concept of leadership seems to loom too large, yet it can actually be achieved by anyone who wants to become one.

In Chapter 1, you will walk through the initial steps and learn how to safely and successfully become the leader your students, teachers, and programs need you to be. It starts by guiding you through the core question, "Why be a leader?" that underlies the resistance to undertaking the challenge. One by one, you will eliminate the barriers you have erected, including the fears you have about taking on the role. By looking at the qualities of a leader, you will discover you have much within you already that you can use as you move onto a larger stage.

Chapter 2 reviews mission and vision statements, which I have discussed in previous books and are central to keeping you grounded when daily demands pull you in multiple directions. You will find suggestions on time management and how to deal with procrastination—the "thief of time" that happens to everyone (and thanks to the Internet, in so many easy ways).

Chapter 3 deals with managing classes in the library, which is a little-recognized challenge. Unlike a classroom, many people come into the library every day. Students come with their entire class or drop in as individuals to do work, teachers come looking for information or a quiet spot, and administrators might walk in with guests at any time. You might have parent volunteers to coordinate. If you are struggling to keep noise to an acceptable level, yelling at students for one reason or another, or having difficulty settling a class down, you will be judged as being incapable of managing the library.

Chapter 4 explores becoming an expert teacher, since you will be judged on that basis by your colleagues and administrators. Even if you started out as a classroom teacher, the library environment is radically different. What worked when the students were "yours" does not always translate when classes come in and out, and you don't have the implied power of grades.

With these basics in hand, you are ready to fully step into leadership.

CHAPTER ONE

WHY BE A LEADER?

When the first Elementary and Secondary Education Act (ESEA) was passed in 1965, administrators scrambled to hire librarians, frequently encouraging teachers to get emergency certification. Closets were turned into libraries to meet requirements of the act and benefit from the sums of money the Federal government was giving schools. The money dried up over time. Librarians complained about tight budgets, but everyone had become accustomed to school libraries and librarians as being part of the school community.

National standards encouraged having multiple librarians when school populations reached over 1,000. At the elementary level, principals discovered they could use librarians along with art, music, and physical education teachers to cover duty-free periods guaranteed in teacher contracts. High-school libraries and librarians were required as part of regional accrediting agencies. As long as you didn't cause trouble for the administration, you could be assured you would get tenure and remain on the job until you decided to retire. No one worried. Budgets might shrink, but librarian positions were secure. The economic downturn in 2008 turned this way of thinking upside down.

We now have the latest iteration of ESEA. The Every Student Succeeds Act (ESSA) is replacing No Child Left Behind (NCLB). Common Core is being challenged and revised, but some manifestation of it will remain. The pressure to reduce the amount of testing will lessen it to some extent, but it won't disappear. The good news is that not since the original ESEA have libraries and librarians been incorporated into the act, although librarians need to know this and fight for their place within it. This is yet one more reason to step into a role as a leader.

ACCEPTING THE CHALLENGE

Everyone seemed to be stunned when librarians were being eliminated from schools. A lone voice in the wilderness had sounded an early warning but few heeded his message: In 1997, Gary Hartzell wrote an article for the *School Library*

Journal titled, "The Invisible School Librarian: Why Others Are Blind to Your Value."[1] The article addressed the fact that principals did not learn about the role of the librarian in their teacher or administrator training, and librarians were not visible in nonlibrary organizations. Librarians sighed in agreement. They were not valued. But, they did nothing to rise to the implied challenge.

Librarians had become complacent. Suggestions would be offered in professional journals on becoming familiar with subject and/or grade curricula. Workshops might encourage them to work collaboratively with teachers. Some librarians responded and found new ways to become involved within the school community. They became building leaders, recognized for their contributions to students, teachers, and even administrators.

Far too many librarians decided the effort was just not worth it. After all, they had tenure and no one was complaining. Elementary librarians pointed out that their jobs were guaranteed, since they were contractually bound to cover teacher free time and by default, needed.

Then the economy crashed. School budgets were slashed. It soon was apparent that no one was safe. Administrators hungry for every dollar looked at library budgets and staffing, and saw a quick fix. No one knew exactly what the librarian did. Why spend precious money on a program and person no one thought was very important? Although the Great Recession was the major factor, librarians had contributed to their own misfortune. By staying within the four walls of their facility and not becoming vital to teachers, they were truly invisible.

When push came to shove and teachers were looking at increased class sizes, they had no reason to rally to the defense of the librarian. If the position had been kept open, their classes would have been even larger. Why bother? Librarians do nothing more than check out books. Volunteers could do the same job, if necessary. Besides, many teachers now had classroom collections, and there was the Internet. Anyone could use Google and Wikipedia to get all the answers at the click of a mouse. Who needed a librarian?

Across the country, libraries were decimated. Where libraries and librarians weren't completely eliminated, they were stretched to cover several schools, and in the largest schools, they would be left with a single librarian to cover a huge load of students. All this was happening as changes in technology accelerated and librarians scrambled to keep current.

That historical review brings us to where we are today. Although the elimination of positions and programs is still happening, the pace has slowed considerably, and in some places, librarians have been restored. But the climate has changed irrevocably.

The bad news litany is complete. The past can't be changed. But we can and must learn from it to be certain it isn't repeated. The present is certainly far from perfect, but there is time to make the necessary changes.

You can no longer be complacent about your future. You must take responsibility to ensure that you will not be overlooked again. And the only way to do that is to become a leader. In short, leadership is not an option—it is a job responsibility.

Few of you learned how to lead while in library school, and those who did found the task much more complex when confronted by a heavy work load, pressure from high-stakes tests, and teacher resistance to working with you. You might have looked with awe at some of the incredible programs some school librarians have created. The thought that you could do anything similar seems beyond the realms of what is possible.

Fear not. You are to be congratulated for having accepted the challenge of learning how to lead despite internal and external constraints. You and your program are not going to change overnight, but you are going to move into leadership in incremental steps. With each one, you will gain more confidence, become clearer in the direction you want to go, and move from being invisible to be perceived as indispensable.

ROADBLOCKS TO LEADERSHIP

Librarians love to tell stories. Story is at the heart of fiction. At the elementary level, librarians read stories to students to connect them to our literary heritage, begin building a love of reading, and attune them to the sound of English and the magic of language.

Stories are wonderful—except for the stories we tell ourselves. Many of you have told yourself stories to explain why you aren't a leader and can never be one. Until you look at them closely and realize they are just stories, you won't be able to move forward.

"I Don't Have Time."

This is one of the most common stories we tell ourselves. We use it often for many things, but when you use it to explain why you aren't leading, it stops you in your tracks. Like any fiction, it is grounded in some truth. You have a very demanding schedule. Your workday begins the moment you open the library doors and doesn't end until you close them. When work is over, you have a host of other obligations that keep you busy often until you go to bed. You obviously have no time to lead.

The truth you are not facing is no one *has* time. We all live at full speed. You must *make* time. And the only way you can do that is by deciding something is a priority in your life. For example, one of your children becomes active in a sport. This requires taking him or her to practice and back home. It means you will *make* time to watch games and perhaps learn more about the sport than you previously knew—or cared about. It became a priority in your life, and you figured out how to make it work.

The same is true with becoming a leader. Once you realize that being a leader is important for getting everyone in the school more aware of the library program and why it is indispensable, you are ready to begin taking the steps to become one.

Oddly enough at the beginning, being a leader won't take much time. You will look for ways to showcase your program and make it visible. You will do more to connect with teachers and others, but really that has always been a component of your job. Now you will do it with greater focus. Only when you step up to leading on the state and national level will it take up a significant amount of time. At that point, you will also see that the returns you get more than outweigh what you have given up by making the time commitment.

"Leaders Are Born."

Another common story, this is also a partially true statement. You can look at a kindergarten class and pick out the leaders. Other kids naturally seem to follow them. You look at yourself by contrast and know that you never have been a leader. You just weren't born that way.

It is easy to be a leader if you do have that instinctive bent, but that doesn't mean you cannot become one. From personal experience, I have learned that *anyone* can become a leader. All it takes is willingness.

I was not a leader when I was in school. As a matter of fact, when I was in high school I was definitely among the "outsider" kids. I wasn't asked to certain parties nor did I hang around with the "in" crowd. I wouldn't have had the first idea how to do it. I didn't do much better in college.

After I graduated, my first job was as a high-school librarian with an emergency license, while I worked toward getting my master's degree. Frankly, I was terrible, and I wasn't rehired. I got another job in a school where there was a more experienced librarian. I learned a lot from her, but when she left the next year, I was unprepared to deal with a very difficult new boss and quit mid-year. Obviously, anyone could tell I had no leadership skills.

It was only when I returned to the workforce after my children were in school that I began to become a leader. Being a librarian in a brand-new elementary school designed on the British Infant School model, I needed to create a library program where there hadn't been one. All of us were charting new territory. My teacher colleagues, fortunately, were all open to trying new things.

I began having successes. I took courses for a supervisor's certificate and in the process met other librarians in my state who were leaders or on the path to leadership. My first book, *The Elementary School Librarian's Almanac,* was an outgrowth of that course. I attended my state conference and joined committees. Eventually, I became active in AASL, extending into ALA committees. I knew leaders from around the country. I recognized my own expertise, and my vocabulary became fluent in expressing to others the value of school library programs. I had thoroughly evolved into being a leader.

While the specifics of my story are unique, the path is similar to that of many others. First, you become successful in your building. You do things and get involved in projects that make your colleagues and administrators realize that you can make an important contribution. Your confidence grows. You try more.

Hopefully, you begin to participate at the state and national levels.

It's not an overnight transformation. It's a steady path of growth. One day you realize you have written a new story about yourself. This time, you are a leader.

"I'm Too Introverted to Be a Leader."

This story includes the variant, "I can't speak in front of a crowd. I freeze up." You are not alone. Studies show many people are less afraid of death than public speaking. So this part is true.

What you are ignoring is you don't have to address an audience to be your building's leader. As a matter of fact, you will always do best by speaking one-on-one with people. And being an introvert can be an asset. Most introverts are good listeners. Extroverts can't wait to talk, and that's not the best way to communicate with others.

As you will learn, communication and relationships are the path to leadership. Neither one requires you to leave your comfort zone as an introvert. There are other places where you probably will feel somewhat challenged, but you will get there in small increments.

One day, after you are fully comfortable in your role as a leader, you might even find yourself speaking to the parent-teacher group at your school. You might feel a bit wobbly, but you will be so secure in your knowledge and be so eager to explain what the library program is doing for their children, you will get past it. You might even do a presentation for your state conference. Yes, it's a long way off from where you are now, but once you take the first steps to leadership, you never know where it will take you.

Now that you realize your roadblocks are mainly caused by the stories you have told yourself, see what other negative stories you have permitted to become barriers for you. Start telling yourself new stories—positive ones.

QUALITIES OF A LEADER

You can find many leadership qualities if you do an online search. Some of them might seem beyond you at this time. Others you already have. This is a basic list with which to begin. We will expand on it as we go along and repeat some as new aspects of leadership are introduced. In this way, you will become familiar and comfortable with them.

Integrity

This is not usually placed first, but it's a very important quality. You must be trustworthy if you are going to be a leader. No one wants to work with, let alone follow, someone they can't trust.

If you have made your library a welcoming environment, teachers will drop in often. You can encourage this by keeping food and coffee available. When they are there, they naturally will talk. Sometimes it's about nothing much. Other times they might complain or rant about another teacher, an administrator, a parent, or a student.

You need to be very careful. While it's important to be sympathetic, you never want to agree with what they are saying. If they repeat your support—and they will—it will damage your reputation. On the other hand, you must not tell anyone what they have said.

The same is true when a teacher imparts a confidence to you. I have had teachers tell me very personal details of their lives. There is something about the library that seems to invite it—perhaps because, while you are a colleague, you are not one of the teachers in their department or grade level. You feel safe. And you must be.

Holding confidences makes a connection. It's not always easy to know these details, but it is far better for you to keep them to yourself. In doing so, you will build your reputation for integrity and trustworthiness, while adding another building block to being recognized as a leader.

Team Player

It might seem contrary to logic to list team player as a leadership quality, but think of migrating birds. One takes the lead for a stretch, and then falls back and follows the new leader. You won't take turns, but sometimes you will be in the lead, and other times you are part of the team.

You want your administration to see you as a team player. If you aren't a team player, you are an obstacle, and you certainly don't want to be viewed *that* way. This is not to say you want to be seen as being a "brown-noser." What you need to do is listen carefully for what the administrator wants to achieve and think of ways the library program can advance it.

For example, the administration at the high school where I was working wanted to go to block scheduling. Although they claimed to want to hear from the teachers, I quickly realized it was a foregone conclusion. Their goal was to change the method of instructional delivery, ending the practice of teachers lecturing for an entire period.

Moving from a 45-minute period to 90 minutes would effectively do that. Despite the efforts to convince teachers, many departments remained opposed to it. What I did was locate resources to help teachers manage under the new arrangement. I spoke with the administrators and was given extra money to purchase these items, so they would be available as soon as possible. Then I worked with teachers, pointing out that the decision was made but the library had material to help them devise lessons that would work with the new schedule.

The other "team" you are on is the one with the teachers. As librarians, we often complain that we are not viewed as teachers, despite the fact that we teach so much of the time. If you want teachers to view you as one of them, be careful to speak inclusively. Always say, "we teachers" as a reminder that you are on the same team. It will help.

In Chapter 4, you will learn more about how to be a team player. It's not nearly as difficult as you might suspect.

Sense of Humor

This quality of leadership is not always mentioned, but it is well worth thinking about. The stresses of Common Core Standards, PARCC testing, concerns about ESSA changes, and the unease created by tight budgets have led to a negative climate in many schools. It's easy to find something to complain about and criticize. Many feel—for good reason—that the joy has been taken out of teaching.

You have the same pressures, and the economic situation often puts your job in jeopardy more than that of teachers, but coming in each day with a negative attitude will not help. Good leaders take their work seriously but themselves lightly.

Sometimes the humor is of the M*A*S*H variety. You just laugh at the craziness of what is happening. Although misery might love company, constantly talking about what is wrong with education today doesn't make anyone feel better.

Putting a positive spin on life in the trenches will bring more of your colleagues to you than joining in on complaint sessions. This doesn't mean you trivialize what is happening. You need to be real, but look for good things to focus on. Share funny memes from Facebook or other sources. This can be the easiest quality for you to exhibit.

Visionary and Risk Taker

Leaders see the big picture, which allows them to have a vision for the future. You may not think you have a vision, but you do have a larger perspective on the education program than the classroom teacher. On the most basic level, this is because you see students over several years and watch them grow. You also deal with students at different grade levels and/or subject areas, giving you an awareness of what happens throughout the educational experience of students.

In addition, you interact in large or small ways with virtually all teachers. You may have parent volunteers who bring you a sense of what the community thinks. Guests are invariably brought to the library, most often accompanied by the principal, and you get to hear what he or she thinks is important about your program and possibly the educational experience of students.

You should have a vision statement for your library program. Chapter 2 discusses the importance of it and how to craft one if you don't have one. Even if you do, what you learn might show you some new aspects of what the statement needs to be and encourage you to tweak or rewrite the one you have.

Because leaders have vision and see the big picture, there are times when they are also innovators. Innovation can be a risk, as there will always be those who don't want change or the innovation doesn't work as planned. Being a risk taker is one reason many librarians don't want to be leaders. It is scary. A risk carries with it the possibility of failure. If it were impossible to fail, it wouldn't be a risk.

For the time being, just accept it as one single element of leadership. By going in small incremental steps, you will see that you need not take this on immediately. When you do, the risks will be small ones. Slowly, you will build your confidence and reputation, so you will be in a good position to take on larger challenges.

MEASURING UP

There are many more qualities of a leader, and we will explore them. You will be surprised to discover you have many of them. You can also develop the ones that you feel you don't have.

The list of leadership qualities, while far from complete, might seem daunting, but reflect on them for a moment. Integrity was the first one discussed. Do you feel you have that quality? Do your colleagues regard you as trustworthy? How can you tell? If you haven't been as careful as you need to be in guarding the confidentiality of others, start now.

You undoubtedly are a team player to some extent. Most of you have always been careful not to "rock the boat." Now you need to become more conscious of how you can quietly support administrators. For example, many principals want to see more tech integration into the classroom. So do you, and you have the expertise to do it. Some librarians send out weekly e-mails alerting teachers to apps and online resources. To get started, go to the AASL website (www.ala.org/aasl) and click on the tabs labeled "Best Apps for Teaching and Learning" and "Best Websites for Teaching and Learning." You will find a host of possibilities.

If teachers begin using one or more of your suggestions, let your principal know. But don't focus on you: Highlight the fact that the teacher tried it and is using the resource with students. This serves two purposes. If and when the principal lets the teacher know he or she is aware of the tech integration and is glad to see it, the teacher will recognize that you were the one to put him or her in a favorable light. At the same time, the principal is aware you were the one responsible for it.

Having vision and taking risks might seem beyond your current scope, but that is not completely true. Think of your facility. Have you been making any changes to it? Perhaps you have rearranged the furniture. Have you instituted a schoolwide reading program? Don't minimize the small things you have done. Each of those required some vision and entailed a degree of risk. It didn't have to be huge.

If you haven't done something like that, consider what you might try. Would the art teacher want to display student work in the library? If so, you can post the information on your library website. Your principal is sure to notice, and once again, you have spotlighted a teacher. Slowly, you can build your ability to take risks, and as you do, you also become more visible, which is a key factor in being a leader. Obviously, leaders don't hide within the four walls of their room.

Can you think of other leadership qualities? Look at a leader in the library field or a teacher leader in your building. What makes them leaders? What do they do? How do they behave and interact with others? Try to identify the qualities they possess and see how close you come to having them as well.

FEAR FACTOR

You might be thinking you will never be able to lead because you have too much fear of making a mistake and all the possible dire consequences of that. The good (and bad) news is that leaders are also afraid at times. Making huge changes, taking on challenges outside your comfort zone, and putting yourself out front makes everyone feel exposed and aware that not everything works.

The bottom line is that most mistakes are usually most obvious to the one who made them. In the course of my career, I led two library renovation projects and was among the first to automate my library. I was completely out of my comfort zone with all of them and a lot of money was involved.

For the automation project, I used my contacts with colleagues I had met at AASL conferences who had already led the way. With their advice, I crafted an RFP to get bids on the project and even figured out (with their help) how to phrase it, so that the vendor I wanted (who had been highly recommended) would get the bid. The same sources helped me determine what I needed for my file server and circulation desk computer. (At the early stage, we couldn't afford many computers. My file server alone, which was pitifully small compared to today's models, was over $9,000.) Once the vendor was selected, I had access to their expertise in completing the project.

The two renovation projects were far outside anything I had ever done. The first was the construction of an addition to the school. I had to work with an architect and the various contractors. While I caught the absence of sufficient outlets for the workroom, I missed the placement of the circulation desk over a floor outlet, which subsequently required altering plans somewhat since the checkout desk covered the outlet needed for the computer. Did I get into trouble? Absolutely not. So much was being done and the results were looking so spectacular, it was barely noticed. I, of course, was aware of my mistake and was upset about it for a while.

The second renovation aimed to increase shelf and floor space in a library that couldn't be physically expanded. My superintendent thought movable stacks for the collection would be a good idea. Team player that I am, I went along with it. I contacted a company I knew from a conference exhibit and they drew up a plan that could be divided over three years.

I knew from my first project that I wanted more flexibility, so I had casters on all the tables. Wireless technology was still in the future, so the tables had grommets for future computers to plug into the many floor outlets. We also had an area for computers for when whole classes used the library. My big mistake was the grommets. They were supposed to lie completely flat. They didn't. Worse, it was too easy to remove, so the kids did. I eventually took out all of them. That left "holes" in the table that my male students soon saw as perfect for a game. They would flick a mini-paper ball to see if they could "score" by having it drop into the hole at the opposite end of the table. As long as they weren't disruptive, I allowed it. It was part of making the library a welcoming environment, and they didn't do it while working on projects.

No one but me regarded it as a mistake. The superintendent focused on the moveable stacks, which gave us 25 percent more shelf space, and with the changes in furniture, we also picked up about the same increase in floor space. Since the big goals of the project had been achieved, no one complained. Indeed, there was only praise.

The point of the stories is that our fear of failure far exceeds the reality of what happens. It's important to face the small failures and acknowledge them. One of the lessons we want to teach our students is that failing in something is not to be feared. It's part of the learning process. We need to begin learning that ourselves.

KEY IDEAS

- » The growth of school library programs and librarians began with ESEA in 1965 and ended abruptly with the Great Recession in 2008.
- » Few heeded the message of Gary Hartzell's article on "invisible librarians."
- » To some extent, librarians were unwitting participants in their own fate.
- » Leadership is no longer an option. It is a job requirement.
- » Leadership can and must be learned.
- » We tell ourselves stories and then believe them.
- » No one *has* time to lead; we need to *make* time.
- » Although some are born leaders, anyone can become one.
- » Being an introvert can be an asset, not a detriment, to leadership.
- » Integrity is a core leadership quality.
- » Leaders need to be team players.
- » Having a vision and being a risk taker might be scary, but they are necessary for leaders.
- » A sense of humor is an important quality, particularly in today's school environment.
- » Reexamine the list of leadership qualities, and discover that you are on your way to having them.
- » Our fear of failure prevents us from moving out of our comfort zone.
- » When we do make mistakes as leaders, we are usually the only ones who notice or care about them.
- » Making mistakes is part of the learning process.

Note

1. Hartzell, Gary N., (1997). *The invisible school librarian: Why others are blind to your value.* Retrieved from ERIC database (EJ554171)

CHAPTER TWO

GETTING GROUNDED

Challenges and new ideas came your way in Chapter 1. The concept of leadership and becoming one is intimidating. At this early stage, you are likely to believe this is still an impossible goal. Too much is swirling in your head, making clear thinking difficult.

In a way, this is very similar to what happens to school librarians every day. Unlike classroom teachers, for you change is a constant. At the elementary level, classes arrive, you deliver a lesson and/or read a story, students check out books and leave, and then another class arrives. If you have any breathing room, you try to catch up with checking items in and shelving them, as well as completing clerical tasks. You might have volunteers, but they need frequent direction from you. You rarely have a moment to think.

At the secondary level, if you have a busy library, you are likely to have multiple classes in at the same time along with "drop-in" students. Most high schools have several lunch periods, so you might have kids who use the library at that time while you are also seeing classes. Teachers come in with questions or to schedule their classes. You get as much information as you can about what their students will be doing and find out whether or not the teacher wants you to introduce the lesson, suggest databases, and/or work with students. Someone is always coming in or going out.

You work hard each day. If you come in early, students are eager to use the library before school, and teachers seeing you are open come in for any of a number of reasons, all of which require your attention. The same is true if you stay late. Finding time to manage the library program is not easy.

By the end of the school year, you are exhausted. You know you worked hard every day, but it's difficult for you to know just what got done, aside from the daily grind. What you need is a way to get grounded and centered.

WHO ARE YOU?

We have taken on so many roles over the years that we suffer from a multiple personality disorder. We began by being called "school librarians." Everything was quite clear. We had a large room with books. Our job was to help students find the books they needed and wanted, either for a school assignment or pleasure reading. We were responsible for ordering appropriate books and magazines, maintaining records including the card catalog, and keeping the facility in order so materials could be easily located.

By the mid-twentieth century we also took care of 16 mm film projectors. At the high-school level, many librarians had an AV club (made up of boys) who set up the projectors for teachers. A library council (all girls) helped with shelving and checked out books. Life was orderly.

In 1969, AASL and NEA Department of Audiovisual Instruction (DAVI) published *Standards for School Media Programs.* Coordinated by Frances Henne, these standards signaled a shift: Print and nonprint materials were to be regarded equally. Librarians were now called media specialists, and our jobs expanded.[1] Over 45 years have passed. Standards have been updated four times since then, the most recent being *Empowering Learners: Guidelines for School Library Media Programs,* published by AASL in 2009. New standards will be published in the fall of 2017.

We were now school library media specialists, showing our added role, but shortly after the 2009 standards were published, AASL decided to revert back to the title of "school librarian." This doesn't take into account the states that call us "teacher librarians" or the librarians who consider themselves "cybrarians," or the few places now identifying us as "innovation specialists." We wear many hats and finding one title to encompass all we do seems impossible.

So who are you? How do you see yourself? How many roles do you play in your school? *Empowering Learners* lists four roles: teacher, information specialist, instructional partner, and administrator.[2] Each of these carries a host of responsibilities. Which do you see as most important? Which make you unique within the school community? (This idea of uniqueness will keep coming up.)

You need to understand your roles—how you fit in and the ways you transform the school community. Think of what would be lost if your program disappeared. As you move through the succeeding chapters, you will discover how to ensure that teachers, administrators, and others will recognize that eliminating the library program would result in a serious loss for students—and everyone else.

MISSION STATEMENTS

In *Being Indispensable* (Toor and Weisburg, 2011) and *New on the Job,* second edition (Weisburg and Toor, 2015), I discussed mission statements. The need for them is so important, it bears repeating from the standpoint of leadership, as well as for structuring your library program. In today's world, every corporation has a mission statement. It becomes a touchstone for all they do.

School districts invariably have a mission statement. Unfortunately, in too many places, no one remembers what it is. A mission statement is your guide when planning anything. Why would you invest time and energy in something that does not advance your mission?

Why It Is Needed

Your mission statement proclaims your purpose—your reason for being. As a school librarian, it underscores what makes you unique and indispensable to students, staff, and as research studies have shown, the entire educational community. It is why you became a school librarian and what you aim to do every day.

When you work with a class, you should have your mission in the back of your mind. Ask yourself, how do I design this lesson so that it furthers my mission in regard to students? When you work with teachers, think of your mission both in how you build the collaborative relationship as well as the best way to present the unit or lesson. In communications with your administration, the mission statement should guide what you say and how you say it.

Earlier, I noted how often school librarians end the year exhausted. Too often they know they worked hard but cannot pinpoint what they accomplished. Without a mission they are rudderless. Their "ship" is pulled this way and that by stray winds and currents. Everyone who comes into the library wanting something blows that ship in another direction. It's no wonder the librarian often feels tired and overwhelmed.

A mission statement grounds and centers you. You can put all requests into the context of whether or not it advances your mission. While you sometimes must do things that don't forward it, you are at least aware that you are temporarily off-course. It will happen frequently during the school year, but you will always know how to get back on track.

Any plans you make and any programs you create must in some way further your mission. Think of your mission as your "perspiration." It defines the core of what you know you are there to do. If you haven't written yours as yet, it is time to do so. If you have one, you need to review it to see if it meets all the parameters and showcases you and your program in the best possible way.

The corporate world has long recognized the importance of a mission statement. Here are some from companies you probably recognize:

> » To care for the world we live in, from the products we make to the ways in which we give back to society. —*Aveda*
> » Provide branded products and services of superior quality and value that improve the lives of the world's consumers, now and for generations to come. —*Proctor & Gamble*

» Committed to providing our customers with the best possible service—and to improving it every day. —*Nordstrom*
» Helping pets live longer, happier, and healthier lives through proper nutrition and care. —*Purina*
» To give people the power to share and make the world more open and connected. —*Facebook*
» To provide personal vehicle owners and enthusiasts with the vehicle related products and knowledge that fulfill their wants and needs at the right price. Our friendly, knowledgeable and professional staff will help inspire, educate and problem-solve for our customers. —*Advanced Auto Parts*

Crafting a Mission Statement

Most librarians start writing their mission statement by looking at the one AASL includes in *Empowering Learners: Guidelines for School Library Media Programs.*

> The mission of the school library media program is to ensure that students and staff are effective users of ideas and information. The school library media specialist (SLMS) empowers students to be critical thinkers, enthusiastic readers, skillful researches, and ethical users of information . . .[3]

It's an excellent way to begin, however the statement goes on to list how this is done. This is not necessary in a mission and makes it too long. You need to be able to memorize it. Not counting the opening phrase of "The mission of the [Blank] Library Program is…" it should be between 25 and 50 words—not any longer. The AASL statement is used and sometimes modified by many school librarians when they write their statements.

Since it appeared over seven years ago, the mission statement already needs tweaking as students need to be more than "users of ideas and information." In today's world, they need to be producers as well. This is a reminder that no matter how good your mission statement is, you do need to revisit it every few years to see if it still meets the definition of your purpose. As I said at the beginning of this chapter, change is a constant in your work life and your mission statement needs to reflect any significant changes.

It is perfectly acceptable to use the AASL mission statement as is, giving credit of course, but you should consider making your mission statement reflect more closely what you consider to be your own purpose. Instead of starting to write it by borrowing what you like from the one in *Empowering Learning,* do a web search under "school library mission statements." In looking at the many examples, you will see some keep the AASL mission intact or vary it somewhat. Others make significant changes.

Some of these mission statements fall within the 25–50-word length, while others go on for over 100 words. They are potentially useful for you. Analyze them and note the words that are repeated regularly. Are there any others that resonate for you? Make a list of all the words and phrases you like.

Here are four more mission statements:

» The mission of the School Library Program is to ensure that students and staff are effective users and producers of ideas and information, to promote literacy, and to develop students' competencies to be ethical participants in a global society.
» The School District Library Program promotes and encourages independent reading, develops critical thinking skills, teaches the effective and ethical use of information sources, and provides equitable access to all forms of information.
» The School Library Program provides a positive environment, encouraging students to love reading, and develops their ability to be critical thinkers, problem solvers, and effective users and producers of ideas, while guiding them to become lifelong learners.
» The School Library Program develops students' ability to be critical readers and thinkers, capable of using information and ideas effectively and ethically, as they create and share new knowledge, and become successful digital citizens in the global marketplace.

Each statement has strengths. All proclaim what is unique about the library program, although they stress different aspects. Since you want your mission statement to be powerful, every word is important. The opening focuses on the skill or area you deem most important. Think about what you consider most significant about your program. What do you want everyone to recognize about it?

Now sit down with your list of words and begin forming them into your own mission statement. Keep your statement in the present tense. Avoid weak words such as "enhance," "enrich," and "support." These are "warm, fuzzies," nice to have, but to administrators making tough decisions, they come across as not vital. "Empower," "integral," "central," and "essential" are much stronger.

Read your newly written statement out loud. Does it sound powerful? Before you settle on it, test your new mission statement with various stakeholders. Ask teachers with whom you have a relationship what they think of it. Did it tell them anything new about your program or confirm what they always knew? Can they think of anyone else in the building who does any of what you included in your statement? If so, you need to make changes. Everything in your mission statement should be declaring how *you* are unique.

If you have parent volunteers, show your statement to them and ask them the same questions. Those of you who work in a middle or high school can test it with some of your "regular" students. Once you think it is fully polished, bring it to your principal and/or supervisor for their feedback. You want to make it as tight and powerful as you can.

What to Do with Your Mission Statement

Now that you have a mission statement declaring your purpose, share it widely. Print it in landscape layout using a strong, easy-to-read font such as Ariel in bold. Adjust the font size for the best fit on the page. Frame your statement and hang it in a prominent place on the reading floor of your library. You want everyone who comes into the library to see it.

You mission statement should also be posted on your website. You might briefly explain each of the skills and practices you identified as unique to your program. If you have a special program (such as book fair or author visit) that will be taking place in the library under your auspices and for which you will be sending out announcements, include your mission statement.

Also hang your mission statement in your office and/or near the circulation desk where you (and others) can see it every day. Memorize it. It needs to become a part of you. When the school year ends, look at your mission statement, and reflect on how well your interactions with students and staff were in alignment with it.

As you prepare to return to school in the fall, stop and consider if it still fully encompasses your purpose. As noted earlier, the statement included in *Empowering Learners* appeared in 2009 and didn't include the importance of students becoming producers as well as consumers of information. In a fast-changing world, you want to be sure your mission statement has kept up with the times. You shouldn't tweak it *too* often, but you do want to be sure it isn't neglecting to include any new aspects of how you impact students and the educational community.

VISION STATEMENTS

Many school districts have mission statements, and a sizeable number of librarians do as well, but vision statements are rarer. Even AASL in *Empowering Learners* did not include a vision statement. Yet, when done well, these statements can be energizing.

The thought process needed for creating a vision statement is challenging. With all you have to do, it's easy to feel this is an extra task and not a pressing need. Give it a try. You need not come up with a finished product on your first attempt. It's worth the effort.

Why It Is Needed

Your vision statement is a way to share with others what the library program potentially could be. It describes how you wish to be perceived. It can and perhaps should be jaw dropping.

In your day-to-day world, you are guided by your mission statement, but your vision statement is the always-somewhat-out-of-reach picture of what a perfect library program would look like. If your mission is your perspiration, your vision is your inspiration and aspiration.

Visions energize people. A well-crafted statement can open people's eyes and show them something they had never considered. When done well, it can make others want to be part of seeing that envisioned future become a reality.

Two classic vision statements best explain the power they have. On May 25, 1961, in an address to Congress on "urgent national needs," President John F. Kennedy said, "I believe that this nation should commit itself to achieving the goal, before this decade is out, of landing a man on the moon and returning him safely to Earth." The idea ignited the imagination of the country. As the program got under way and astronauts were selected, the nation followed it all with high interest.

In 1980, Bill Gates shared his vision of "a computer on every desk and in every home." That sounded completely unrealistic in a time when the personal computer was only a few years old. He actually said it somewhat differently in 1977 when Microsoft was only two years old. He included the words "running Microsoft software" as the company wasn't making computers. The vision energized the company and attracted the attention of others in what was then a fledgling field. Many couldn't believe most people would want computers, but those who did would be the ones who led the way.

Here are some corporate and nonprofit vision statements:

» Helping people around the world eat and live better. —*Kraft Foods*
» To be the number one athletic company in the world. —*Nike*
» We will become the world's most valued company to patients, customers, colleagues, investors, business partners, and the communities where we work and live. —*Pfizer*
» To provide access to the world's information in one click. —*Google*
» Every person has the opportunity to achieve his/her fullest potential and participate in and contribute to all aspects of life. —*Goodwill*
» A just world without poverty. —*Oxfam*
» Our vision is a world in which every child attains the right to survival, protection, development and participation. —*Save the Children*

Compare these vision statements with the sample mission statements. The vision statements portray a highly desirable but not yet achieved future. While there is a difference in tone between the corporate and nonprofit visions, all convey an excitement at what might be achieved if everyone worked to make it happen.

Corporations and schools often blur the distinction between mission and vision, but you will achieve much more if you recognize they are not the same. The samples are specifically chosen to highlight their differences.

Crafting a Vision Statement

The samples from the corporate and nonprofit world give you an idea about vision statements, but now you need to turn your mind to what that looks like for school libraries. You don't have a vision statement from AASL to get you started, so to move you into thinking about what you would want to include, here are some vision statements from schools of library and information studies:

   » SLIS envisions a global society in which information resources are created, protected, managed, and used for the good of society, including addressing challenges and opportunities in the service of equity and productivity for individuals and communities. —*College of Arts, School of Library & Information Studies: The University of Oklahoma http://slis.ou.edu/vmgo*
   » The Simmons College School of Library and Information Science imagines an interconnected world with a diverse and engaged citizenry empowered by information, cultural heritage, and technology; in which the information disciplines and creativity improve lives; and where literature, knowledge, and collective wisdom are preserved and celebrated. —*Simmons College School of Library and Information Science www.simmons.edu/academics/schools/school-of-library-and-information-science/about/mission-vision-objectives*
   » A society which honours institutions that foster individual opportunity to engage with the world of imagination, information, and ideas for learning, citizenship and connecting communities. —*University of Alberta, School of Library and Information Studies https://uofa.ualberta.ca/education/departments/school-of-library-and-information-studies/about-us/slis-mission-statement*

Are there words in these statements that resonate with you? Copy them down to get your thinking started. As with mission statements, visions need to be brief. Don't worry about it now, but you will want to keep your statement between 25 and 50 words, not counting the opening phrase of "The vision of the [Blank] Library is. . . ."

Many years ago, the supervisor of the school library program in an inner city brought her librarians to visit my school. She thought it would be impossible for them to develop a great program unless they saw one in action. You can't envision what you don't know. How can you picture the exciting world you would want to bring to your students and faculty, when all you see is your own school setting?

Use the Internet to search out exemplary school libraries. A notable one is the learning commons designed for the Chelmsford (MA) High School by Valerie Diggs. Her SlideShare presentation (www.slideshare.net/valeriediggs/from-library-to-learning-commonsnyslideshare) gives an excellent overview of how you can move your library to a learning commons. Just contemplating it will give you ideas for your vision.

Search under "learning commons" and the grade level at which you work for more examples. As always, some websites are better than others. Also search under "images." If you enjoy doing it, print out the images that most excite your imagination and create a "dream board" of the library you would like to have.

Here are some sample school library vision statements:

» The school library is the hub of the school, giving students and staff unlimited access to the print and technological resources that meet their needs for today *and* tomorrow.
» The School Library Program is a collaborative partnership between students, teachers, school librarians, administrators, and the community, where print and technological resources allow all to achieve their goals.
» The School Library Program is the heart of the educational community. Love of the written word and research skills for intellectual and personal achievement are grown and nurtured here.
» The School Library Media Program is a user-centered environment where up-to-date resources and technology and a responsive staff empower students and teachers to achieve their academic and personal goals.

These are not the most dramatic of visions but they go beyond a mission. Review all the library-related vision statements. Close your eyes and imagine what your program would look like in an all-perfect world. What would it feel like to those entering? What great things are happening there?

To help you along briefly write your philosophy of a library program and the role of a school librarian. Since your philosophy is based on your beliefs, refer to the common beliefs that open the *AASL Standards for the 21st-Century Learner*.[4] To the list you have started, add words that you feel would most convey the impact of your ideal school library program. Start forming them into one or two sentences. Keep those sentences in the present tense, as doing so makes your statement more powerful.

In library school, you undoubtedly learned Ranganathan's Five Laws of Librarianship. They are as valid today as when he wrote them. Michael Gorman, however, came up with five new laws that parallel and reinforce them.[5] For example, Ranganathan's first law is "Books are for use," while Gorman's is "Libraries serve humanity." Ranganathan's fifth law is "The library is a growing organism," and Gorman ends with "Honor the past and create the future." Read the meaning underlying both sets of laws. You can draw on some for your nission while others will work well in your vision.

Even more than with a mission statement, every word of your vision statement is important. You want to portray your vision of what the library program can bring to everyone in the school. It should be not only *your* inspiration; it should also capture the imagination of *others*.

Creating a vision isn't easy, but it's worthwhile. Your first vision statement doesn't need to be earth shattering, but it should be more uplifting than your mission statement. Consider how you could improve the samples. Play with the sample words as well as the ones you chose, and form them into one or two sentences. Short is best, but it can range from 25 to 50 words.

Live with your creation for about a week. Look at it every so often. Does it make you want to raise the level of your library program—even if you cannot figure out how to do it? Does it inspire you?

When you think it is as good as can be, share it with those close to your library program. See what the teachers who frequent your library think of it. Try it out on any parent or student volunteers you have. At the high-school level, your regular student users can also be asked for their input. If you have come close, you should get at least some "wows."

What to Do with Your Vision Statement

The possibility of achieving your vision will keep you going on the tough days. That is why it's your inspiration. Memorize it so you can keep it in mind. Share it with your administrator, letting him or her know about the possibilities and what you are working to achieve. You don't expect the vision to be realized in the near future, but it's where you want to be heading.

Print your vision statement in landscape layout, frame it, and hang it up next to your mission statement. Look at what you have done. With your mission statement, you have communicated to the world what you do for students, staff, and administration each day. With your vision statement, you let them know you are not resting on your laurels but are always looking to make your program the best it could possibly be.

Post your vision statement above your mission statement on your website. When promoting a library program with parents and/or community members, include it along with your mission. Hold onto your vision as you leave for summer break. Embrace it when you return in the fall. Does it still inspire you? Have you experienced something over the summer that gave you an idea that would make your program have an even greater impact? If so, consider revising your vision statement. The future is ever changing, and you want to change with it.

PROCRASTINATION—THE GOOD, THE BAD, AND THE UGLY

In discussing the stories we tell ourselves, the first one was "I don't have time." It is the most common reason given for not being a leader, and yet, almost everyone wastes time. Often attributed to Charles Dickens, it was actually Edward Young who said, "Procrastination is the thief of time."[6] But procrastination isn't all bad.

With the heavy workloads carried these days, time management is an important skill to develop. Librarians as well as teachers feel stressed, overwhelmed, exhausted, and unappreciated. There are only 24 hours in a day, and as such, it becomes important to maximize the available hours and minutes. Too often this translates into trying to multitask and cram as much work as possible into every spare moment—and there is none to spare. Yet hours are spent on Facebook playing Candy Crush. What is happening here?

When you push yourself to exhaustion, your brain rebels and you wind up doing mindless tasks. You then beat yourself up over having wasted all that time. In reality, you needed it—perhaps not for as long as you spent on Facebook, but necessary all the same. It was wasted time, because you didn't get to appreciate your break, and now you feel bad about what you did.

Procrastination isn't bad when it is *planned*. The bad and the ugly form of procrastination comes when you are so overtired or highly stressed, you zone out and have no awareness of how long you have been playing one game or another. This is why you are so upset with yourself.

Going from one type of task to a very different one is hard on the brain. It can't switch gears that radically. Students cope with this every day when their schedule has them moving from math to history. The two subjects require very dissimilar thinking. Making the shift is difficult. When you recognize what you are doing—learning to select the most suitable task for the time available—you are in charge of time rather than having it drive you. Then you will also know when your brain needs a break and can logically allow it to happen for as long as you deem appropriate. Your game becomes a scheduled relaxation and you can enjoy it.

Take a moment to consider why and when you procrastinate. In addition to what I have mentioned, you might also be trying to avoid certain tasks. Identify the reason why you are dodging them. It might be because they seem so huge, you think they will never get done. Or, you might be uncertain of the best way to tackle them. Or, perhaps you don't think you know enough to do the job.

Each of those possibilities requires a different solution, but procrastinating never gets you there. That's the really ugly side. If the task is too large, see how it could be broken down into more comfortable "bites." Maybe you can get help doing part of it.

When you are uncertain of how to proceed with a task, remove yourself. Perhaps go for a walk. Look at houses, people, or whatever is in your view. Every so often, consider the task. Away from your computer without the clutter of your office and with no students or staff coming to talk to you, you can let your mind roam. Possibilities will occur to you. You can turn them over in your head, put them aside for a moment, go back to observing the world around you, and then return to the ideas you are developing. In the course of a 45-minute walk, you most probably will gain a good handle on how to tackle the task.

If you feel you don't know enough to do a job, for many reasons you might not want to ask people in your school. You are the librarian. You are supposed to know everything—or know how to find it. And you really do. It doesn't have to be a web search. Reach out to colleagues. Post your question on your state association's electronic discussion board. Ask the library "experts" you follow on Twitter. As a group, we are incredibly helpful to one another.

If you find that, aside from your teaching responsibilities, you are taking care of "stuff" that has popped up unexpectedly or fixing things you thought you had taken care of, you are wearing yourself out. Your major tools are a fire extinguisher and duct tape. This is where your mission statement comes in and why it grounds you.

Another common time waster comes from working hard without a focus. The business world has long been aware of the 80:20 rule known as Pareto's Principle. The Internet has numerous sites that explain its application in different situations. For example, corporations and organizations know that 20 percent of the people do 80 percent of the work. In this case, it means that 80 percent of unfocused work results in only 20 percent of work getting done while 20 percent of focused effort results in 80 percent of the work. You can see where being focused on what and why you are doing something will produce big results.

Start by seeing where those seemingly extraneous tasks can fit within your mission by giving them a purpose and focus. If they don't fit, consider why they are occurring and how you can reduce the number of them. Better yet, rethink whether they are an immediate priority or if they need to get done at all.

To-Do Lists

Many people resist the idea of a to-do list, but it can work if you find an approach that works for you. The classic way is to do a daily list. However, it becomes frustrating if you make it too full to get it all done.

Yes, you can shorten the list, but you are likely to think about the items you left off. Instead, don't put a date on top. Mark it "Current." The idea is not to cross them *all* off in one day—just a lot of them. It might take two days or it could take a week to get most of the tasks accomplished. Indeed, following this form, many people prefer a weekly to-do list.

A variation is to categorize the list into your different responsibilities. Divide the list into two columns, with the one on the left taking one-fourth to one-third of the space. In that left-hand column, you might have categories such as "classes," "meetings" (informal or formal), "back room," "tech stuff," and "other." The categories are yours to determine.

Review your list. Is it do-able? How many days would it take to complete? Be honest. Facing reality will help keep you from being overwhelmed. Once you have everything noted, highlight the ones with the highest priority. You will want to get these tasks done first, although you might be doing some minor ones along with the major. More on this in a bit.

Another reality is that, even with all your planning, sometimes a "crisis" interrupts what could have been done. What you should not do is go into panic mode and grab your fire extinguisher or duct tape. Instead, take a moment to decide how high a priority the task really is. Do you have to fix it completely or can you just get it under control?

Accept the fact you don't have control over everything that happens in a school day. Even what happens in your library is not always in your control. Consider keeping an online diary where you can record the date, the crisis, and the time it took to handle it. It might help you anticipate what could go wrong in the future.

Fitting the Task to the Time

To maximize the work you can get done, recognize the different nature of your tasks and then select a job based on how much time you have available. One of the worst things you can do is start working on something that takes an hour or more when you have only 15 minutes available. You will have to stop early, and when you get back to the task, you will need to begin again because you lost the thread of what you were doing.

If you have a few spare minutes, perhaps 15 or less, you can open mail. Drop junk mail in the trash and make a note on the envelope if it needs an action on your part. You can do a quick scan of e-mails, getting rid of the ones you don't need to read and checking on any that might be important. Do *not* get deeply involved. You only have 15 minutes. Grab an armload of books that need to be shelved or, if you do it, check in some books. Elementary librarians can review the stories they are planning to read to students.

When you have 30 minutes to work, you can prepare a simple purchase order or pull books for a teacher for an incoming class. You can also prepare webliography for the class. Weed one or two shelves, and put the books on cart for records to be deleted later. Keep track of which shelves you have weeded. Deleting records is another 30-minute task. Reviewing new books to see if they need any special classification can be done within half an hour. Depending on how complex it needs to be, you can create a lesson plan. You can update your website, and if it's not too extensive, you can do a LibGuide.

Then there are the tasks that require close to one hour or more. Preparing a pathfinder takes focused time. Shifting shelves needs this longer slot (you might need to do some shelf-relabeling as well); any less and you will be caught in the middle of the project when your time is up. You can't do a good job on a quarterly or annual report in short spurts. Give yourself enough time so it is a polished job. If you write them, blog posts will take an hour or more.

Make one more list of the various jobs you do. Analyze them and decide how long they take and whether or not you can return to them easily if you are interrupted. With that list in hand, you will be able to fit these jobs into your available time and get much more accomplished.

One pitfall in time management comes from e-mail, texts, and various social media. Most of us find them addictive on some level. If you are not careful, these tasks can drain all your time. Find a time slot that you can devote to them, and *stick to it.*

Now that you have time-management tools, beware of perfectionism. It can be another barrier to leadership. Nobody does everything right every day—not even the best leaders—and life happens. You will make mistakes. Learn from them, and then make new ones.

No one can do it all, and two heads are better than one. When possible, find partners. Delegate where possible.

And remember to recharge your brain. Some procrastination is good. You just must be mindful of when you really need something completed and how much time to allow for completing it. The better you get at time management, the easier it will be to find time to be a leader—and lead better.

KEY IDEAS

- » Change is a constant in librarians' lives, and keeping up is a challenge.
- » Once libraries became more than just a place for books, we started expanding our roles.
- » We have officially gone from school librarian to school library media specialist and back again to school librarian.
- » AASL identifies four major roles for which librarians are responsible.
- » A mission statement proclaims your purpose and what makes you and the library program unique. It is your "perspiration."
- » A mission statement grounds you and helps you focus your teaching and interactions with students and staff.
- » A mission statement should be between 25 and 50 words and be written in the present tense.
- » Select words and phrases from other mission statements that resonate with you, and use them to craft your own statement.
- » Test the power of your draft statement with various stakeholders.
- » Frame your mission statement, and hang it prominently in your library.
- » Post your mission statement on your website and include it with communications to parents and others.
- » Memorize your mission statement.
- » At the end of the year, use your mission statement to assess how well you did.
- » At the beginning of the school year, review your mission statement to see if it needs tweaking.
- » A vision statement is a compelling view of what you hope to achieve and how you wish to be perceived. It is your inspiration and aspiration.
- » Vision statements can energize people with the possibilities of what might be realized, showing what they might never have imagined a library program to be.
- » Use visions of corporate, nonprofit, and library schools to get your thinking started.
- » To help you get ideas, consider the common beliefs from *Empowering Learning.*
- » Vision statements should be short (less than 50 words) and written in the present tense.
- » Get feedback on your vision statement from different stakeholders.
- » Share your vision statement with your administrator to show him or her where you would like to take the library program.

» Frame your vision statement and hang it near your mission statement.

» As with your mission statement, post your vision statement on your website and include it with communications to parents and others.

» Hold onto your vision statement over the summer to remind you to watch for more possibilities of what your program might become.

» In the fall, consider whether or not you need to modify your vision statement so that it best reflects the future.

» Procrastination can be good if you use it wisely to shift gears from one type of task to another.

» Use your mission statement to ground you when you are being pulled in many directions.

» Identify why you are procrastinating and draw on your various resources to get you past it.

» Pareto's Principle says that 80 percent of your unfocused work gets only 20 percent of the tasks done.

» To-do lists can be effective if you use a type that works best for you.

» Tasks vary in the amount of focused time needed to do them. Fit the task to the time available.

Notes

1. Kester, Diane D., *Frances Henne and the Development of School Library Standards*. University of Illinois at Urbana-Champaign. Retrieved from www.thefreelibrary.com/Frances+Henne+and +the+development+of+school+library+standards.-a0125151317.

2. American Association of School Librarians. *Empowering Learners: Guidelines for School Library Media Programs*. (Chicago: American Library Association, 2009), 16.

3. Ibid. 8.

4. Ibid. 12–13.

5. Gorman, Michael. Five Laws of Library Science Then & Now. *School Library Journal*, July 1998, 20–23. http://pacificreference.pbworks.com/f/Gorman+and+Ranganathan.pdf.

6. Bartleby.com www.bartleby.com/100/224.9.html.

CHAPTER THREE

MANAGING CLASSES IN THE LIBRARY

➤ **You might have had years of experience as a classroom teacher before becoming** a school librarian, but your knowledge of how to manage a class does not always transfer to the library. It is rare when someone interrupts a classroom, but people are always walking into the library. When they do, they automatically assess how well you manage the space.

On the one hand, you want your library to be an open, safe, and welcoming environment. Being a strict disciplinarian with rigid rules runs counter to creating that climate. How do you keep the library from getting out of control and still have that positive atmosphere?

If you cannot manage your library, you won't be seen as a leader in the building. By identifying the challenges and developing skills and techniques necessary for a smoothly functioning facility, you take one more step toward being a leader.

THE CHALLENGE—PART 1

Unlike a classroom teacher, your students aren't yours, and they know it. If you are at the elementary level, you probably have a fixed schedule. The teacher drops off his or her class and departs. For the kids, this is almost as good as having a substitute—maybe better. A library is a wide-open space compared to a classroom. There are places where you can disappear. Best of all, the librarian doesn't give you a grade, or if there is one, it's not that important.

You need to be prepared for this, because sooner or later, how you handle these students will get back to their teachers. Since gossip is a constant factor in schools, you can be sure it will be discussed with other teachers who might concur. You want students to let their teachers know they love going to the library because they learn so much or enjoy the books you read to them and recommend for their own reading.

Teachers have parents in their classroom on special days. It's easy to be great for one day. By contrast, you may have volunteers working in the library every day. Your volunteers are committed parents and will be observing how you interact with their child and with others. If you have a bad day and they see it, they may very well report it back to their friends. Some of these volunteers are well known in the school and might have friends on the Board of Education (or are Board members). When they approve of what you do, they can be your greatest champions in the community. When they don't, your reputation will be harmed.

At the middle- and high-school level, the teacher is usually present, but you will have drop-ins who are supposed to be working on an assignment. They may or may not need your attention. If they are unsupervised, these drop-ins can become noisy and, even worse from a teacher's perspective, disrupt any classes attending the library. In the past, you might have had a second librarian or a clerk help monitor these students, but such additional staff has become increasingly rare.

Your principal could appear at any time. The library is a favored spot for taking visitors, so your administrator might be showing guests around the building. The last thing you want is to be coping with an overly noisy library or disciplining a student in a harsh manner.

You have mission and vision statements to ground you and to define what the library and the library program need to be. A quiet library is a thing of the past, which makes the situation more of a challenge. Based on how you see the library functioning, you need to know how much noise you find acceptable—and how to manage the situation when it exceeds those limits. Do you expect student to *always* be on task or will you tolerate some socializing? How much?

If you have been a librarian for some time, reflect on the climate you have created and how well students behave when they are in the library. Each librarian will have a different standard of what is acceptable. To be sure you aren't erring in one direction or another, talk to a teacher you trust. Explain that you want to be sure your library "feels" the way you want it to be. Ask to what extent it sends that message. Is there anything you need to adjust?

I have always had a "vibrant" library at the high-school level. Translation: It was somewhat noisy. However, there were areas of quiet where those who needed it could work. I could also get students back on task easily when they became a little too boisterous by keeping my requests light-hearted and maintaining the friendly tone I considered vital to the program I created. What you do is up to you, as long as your mission and the vision are upheld.

CONTROL VS. MANAGEMENT

Recall what school was like when you attended. Depending on your age, you may have sat at a desk in a row, or you may have experienced a less formal arrangement. Your teacher probably wrote on a chalkboard, used an overhead projector, and ran filmstrips.

School doesn't look that way today. Smart boards have replaced chalkboards and opaque projectors. Many districts have a 1:1 computer and tablet to student ratio, and laptops are everywhere. But despite the more advanced technology, classrooms tend to operate the way they always have.

However, today's students are very different from when you were in school. I am not saying they are *worse*. They are *different*. They have grown up with technology since they were infants, which makes many adults wary. We tend to forget that most of our students were born in the twenty-first century. The twentieth century is ancient history to them.

According to Beloit College's Annual Mindset of Entering Freshman,[1] those graduating from college in 2019 have never known a time without hybrid cars or high definition TV. They have never licked a postage stamp, and they don't see anything special about a "first woman" doing something. For these students, First Respondents have always been heroes (they were very young when 9/11 occurred), Wi-Fi is an entitlement, cell phones are everywhere (and teachers don't know what they are doing on them), e-mail is for formal communication, and texts and tweets are for casual messages.

Their world is digital; their attention is continually diverted by their various devices. They instinctively know how to do things on these devices, and they are more comfortable using their thumbs than writing in cursive. In many ways, they are foreign territory for you. Although these facts are often presented as criticism, they shouldn't be. This is reality, and adults need to deal with it.

An old truism is one source of the problem: "Teachers teach as they were taught, not as they were taught to teach." (And as already noted, despite all the new technology, many classrooms run just as they did in the past.) The corollary to this idiom is, "Librarians run their libraries as they remember them, rather than reflecting the current world." You still hear "no talking," "whispers only," and "no eating." Students are not permitted to borrow a book if they owe dues. Does this approach truly create a warm welcoming environment or is it your attempt to control the environment?

Unlike the past, students are now expected to work in groups. When several groups are working at the same time, noise levels rise. Having to focus on maintaining an indoor voice when they get excited about what they are finding curtails the flow of thoughts. You don't want to have noise levels so high that it prevents them from hearing an important message, but you do have to increase your tolerance for noise.

The other two restrictions are knee-jerk reactions to which you need to give some thought. You can logically restrict food and drink near computers. But if students are expected to clean up after themselves, you are likely to have less food hidden in the stacks. And it means you don't have to explain why it is OK for faculty to eat in the library during gatherings.

As to not permitting students to borrow books when they owe dues, the message you send is that it's more important for students to develop responsibility than to learn to love reading. Also, you are not taking into consideration the problem of kids from divorced homes who might have left the book at one parent's home and came to school from the other parent's home.

Consider the difference between "control" and "manage." When you control, you are exercising authority over someone. When you manage, you are finding the best solutions to a situation. The need to control comes from fear, uncertainty, or insecurity. (Much of the challenges to library material come from a need to control what students read, originating in fear.) Management comes from confidence, acceptance, and tolerance.

Are you looking for "classroom control" or "classroom management?" Being plunged into the responsibility for the library environment is often intimidating for all the reasons previously discussed. From that fear comes the need to control it. Adding to it is the awareness of how different students are and how technologically adept they are. Humans tend to fear what is different.

When you opt to control the library environment, you cannot make it feel safe and welcoming. In order to ensure you get your desired results, you—not students—need to change. You have to develop a new skill set that will enable you to manage your classes and how you interact with students.

New teachers frequently work very hard to gain discipline in their classrooms. They struggle for control. The harder they work, the more discipline problems they have. Great teachers do not control their students. They seem to manage them effortlessly.

If at all possible, observe a great teacher. Observe the flow of the class. See how disruptions are handled. Try to figure out why students comply with directions without making a fuss. Talk with the teacher afterwards about what you observed, and ask any questions you have. Perhaps the teacher will be willing to share some of his/her techniques.

YOUR ATTITUDE LEADS

Without realizing it, you can be creating difficulties for yourself in managing your classes. Your thoughts can take you in positive or negative directions, and unbeknownst to you, those thoughts are being communicated. You might lose a class before it even starts.

As a librarian, you tend to be highly verbal, but it's important to remember that more than half of our communication is nonverbal.[2] Whether it's over 90 percent or just over 50 percent depends on many factors, but whatever number applies to your current situation, your body language and your tone of voice communicate at least as much as your words. By tuning into your nonverbal messages, you will reduce much of your discipline problems.

Consider this situation: One of your most difficult classes is scheduled to come into the library in five minutes. It's time to get ready for the students. Or, this situation: One of your least favorite teachers is bringing in her class. Your lesson is all prepared.

But is your attitude? What are you thinking? A running monologue is probably going through your head. It sounds something like this: "I really don't need this. They are going to be off the wall. I know Tommy is going to be poking at kids to get a reaction. I bet Mrs. Smith is going to disappear into my office and leave me to figure out what to do with her students—and they are not the best as is."

You are unaware that your body has stiffened. You greet the class, but your voice is tight. Your arms are tightly folded. That troublesome class has gotten the message. You can say, "Welcome," but they know you don't really want to see them. They are aware you don't like them.

How do you think they will behave as a result? They will live up or—in this case—down to your expectations. By the time they leave, you will be exhausted, dreading the next time they are scheduled. The teacher you don't like will get the message as well and will be thinking nasty things about you as she disappears into your office to avoid any further contact. You anticipated her correctly and will feel the same way the next time she brings a class.

As the saying goes, "without change, there is no change." And repeating the same action in hope of a different result is a definition of insanity. But how can you change? The class is the class. The teacher is a pain.

What you must change is *your* attitude. In the case of the class, think, "What can I do to make their day better?" Or, "I know Tommy doesn't do well in school. How can I show him that 'every child succeeds in the library?' What might be the perfect book for him?" (Remember Ranganathan's laws and "Every reader his book.") When the class arrives, smile at students individually. Comment positively on something about one or two of them, such as a T-shirt. (Never the same kids each time.) Let Tommy know you have a book you think he'll like. (What he really has been looking for is attention.)

Before the teacher comes in, reflect on how she is viewed by the rest of the staff. Perhaps she has trouble with classroom management or has some serious personal issues. Coming into the library might be her way of shedding some of her burdens. Give her the time she wants. Think, "I am going to get to really know these kids and what motivates them."

When you change your thinking, you change your attitude. When you change your attitude, you change the nonverbal message you send. It will take time until you can do this easily and then make your new attitude an integral part of you. The better you get at it, the more positive results you will see.

RULES AND ROUTINES

Good classroom teachers have routines that give students an "anchor," which keeps them focused for the most part at what they are doing now and what will happen next. Often a sequence of what happens in class—Enter quietly and sit down; Read quietly until class begins; Be respectful of others; When the bell rings, line up quietly; and so on—it is posted where it can be seen, and if the students start getting unruly, the teacher need only to point to what they are supposed to be doing to get them back on track.

It is harder to set up routines in the library environment, but it is particularly important to put them in place at the elementary level. Think of it as a game. Any player or team manager can tell you that you don't play the game the same way at the opening, during the middle, and at the end. Each part has its own pattern. Think of your lessons the same way.

Involve students in the process. At the beginning of the school year, discuss the routines with each class. Ask their opinion of each part, and discuss why these are important.

Elementary teachers typically have "jobs" posted in their classroom with the names of the students assigned to each. The tasks are rotated so every child gets a chance at all of them. The students usually take pride in their responsibilities. You can't have such a chart in the library, but you can accomplish the same results in how you handle the opening phase of a class.

Opening

When a class is scheduled, try to meet students outside the library door so you can manage the opening routine. Smile genuinely as you greet them. Ask one or two of them to be "in charge" of collecting the books being returned and placing them on a cart. Give another student a direction to quietly remind everyone to find a place to sit.

Be sure to use different students for this first part, and don't choose only those who always do well. Everyone deserves to get some special treatment. In some ways, this is better than the job list in a classroom, as students don't know if they will get a task. It does require you to keep track of who has had a chance to do what, but it's worth the effort.

When the last student has entered, see how well they followed directions and thank them for doing so. Thanking is different from complimenting. This is just recognizing good behavior. Compliments are for praising students when they have accomplished something that is a challenge in some way and should always be specific. It's not, "you did a good job," but "I recognize you thought through the best way to do that."

The challenge for you is when a student is disruptive upon entering the library. It's easy to react negatively and say something like, "If you don't know how to behave in a library, you can sit by yourself until the class is over." You can be sure the student will continue to act out, distracting you from what you are doing. You might even send the student to the office, which only shows that you cannot handle the discipline in the library.

Instead, recognize that the behavior very likely has nothing to do with you or the library. Something set the child off, and this is an opportunity to let it out. You might say something like, "I see you have extra energy today. Why don't you be the one to arrange the returned books on the cart?" Or you can say, "It looks as though you are having a bad day. I think what we are doing in the library might make it better." (If the student is in grade K–3, offer Judith Viorst's *Alexander and the Terrible, No Good, Horrible, Very Bad Day*.) Once you have initiated a calm conversation, the routines you established will help get him or her settled.

Too many libraries post rules that are filled with negatives, which sends a restrictive message. Focus on the positive. The best ones I know are: "Respect yourself, respect others, and respect the library." This covers just about every situation. It includes "no roughhousing" and "no running"—and whatever else you might have put into a negative rule. For example, returning books on time is about respecting others.

To complete the opening, you need to get kids from the book return area to where they will be next. There are several ways of doing this. You can say, "Welcome everyone. I am so glad to see you again. Please go to [wherever you want them seated]." A different approach that will get their attention is to take a picture of where you want them to be—at the tables or on the rug for story. Enlarge it, and set it up by the book return area with a sign saying, "Please sit here." Even if you change where you want them to go from one week to the next, the routine stays consistent.

Making the Middle Work

This is the heart of your lesson. It's critical that you transition smoothly to it from the opening, or you will waste valuable learning time in getting students resettled. Once students are in place, set the background for the lesson. Ask an appropriate question relating to what you are going to read or have them do. Avoid any questions that have one-word answers. You want to get them thinking about the topic.

For storytelling sessions, choose books with some connection to one another. You might have several titles featuring bears, or ones that have a common theme such as persistence or believing in yourself. After each book, ask a few questions to see if the class was able to go beyond the simple plot. If they have difficulty, be prepared with guiding questions to help them discover it.

When you have read all the selections, you need to tie them together. Ask what they think all the books were about. Again, you might have to help them along. Then get back to your opening question. In the case of books about persistence, it's not, "What have you been able to do because you worked at it?" although that can be one of the questions you ask—even at the opening. Instead ask them, "What are some benefits of persistence?" When you ask the same question at the end as you did in the beginning, you get them to realize what they have learned—what they will be taking away from the class.

In the next chapter, you will learn more about "essential questions," but for now consider that a research assignment at the elementary or high-school level should have at least one essential question built into it in some way. For example, one class was researching the life of Rembrandt and had to see how the artist's life influenced his work. The teacher thought that was the essential question. Without any other guidance, students wouldn't get much more out of that. They likely will not remember much about that project in a few years.

Instead, the project should conclude with students sharing what each of them has learned, then move on to a deeper discussion where they should talk about the essential question. This might be examining their reaction to the saying that "Art imitates life," and making a personal determination as to whether that is true or whether the reverse —"Life imitates art"—is true. Some might feel that neither statement is accurate, but in working through this, they will get a far deeper understanding of what inspires and affects creative people and to what extent we are all creative in our own ways.

End Game

As any athlete or chess player can tell you, the end game is critical. At the elementary level, the teacher will be taking students back to class. Will students be pushing and shoving as they line up? Will they be talking loudly as the lesson ends? The teacher will judge you on the exiting behavior of the class.

Have a closing routine with which students become familiar. Reserve at least five minutes for this to properly wrap up the class. Exit tickets with questions written on them can be used at many grade levels and are highly effective as a technique not only for ending a class smoothly but also for metacognition, which helps the students remember the most important points of the lesson. With elementary students, you can ask the questions directly and have several students answer each one. Some possibilities are:

» What was the most important thing you learned today?
» What was the best part of class today?
» I was confused about . . .
» What would you like to learn about next?

With older students, you can hand them cards with the tickets to fill out and hand back to you as they leave (hence the reason why they are called "exit" tickets). In addition to the ones above, you can have middle- and high-school students answer any of the following:

» How could you apply this information today—this week—or in a way that might have helped you in the past?
» With one being the worst and 10 being the best, rate your understanding of today's topic. Why do you give it that rating?
» If you could teach someone just one thing about today's lesson, what would it be? Why?
    (Exit ticket ideas were taken from a list developed by Patricia Sarles and shared on the AASL forum Electronic Discussion Board.)

Routines in middle school and high school are different as you get classes coming in with their teachers (along with drop-ins), but you still need them.

Recognize that a class has been traveling in a "pack" through the halls and now is entering the library. You want them to expeditiously move to where the lesson will begin. Unless *you* are there to direct them, *they* will decide where they should go.

In most places, drop-ins need to sign in and present a pass from their teacher. If you don't have a clerk of some type, the step might get skipped. Keep a sign-in sheet in a highly visible location. Have a place for students to leave their pass and then retrieve it for you to sign when they leave. Have them sign out as well. Do the best you can to watch them enter and exit while you work with a class.

Bathroom passes can be another disruption if students need to interrupt you while you are teaching. You can usually laminate two or three passes and hold onto them. When students ask, hand them a pass, but have them sign out on a sheet separate from the sign-in sheet. After they hand you the pass on their return, they should sign themselves back in.

Students hate signing in and out, but you are legally responsible for knowing where they are. Most of them will be reasonable if you explain that to them. It can be particularly important in a fire drill or other situation requiring everyone to leave the building. You must know if you have any students in the bathroom and be able to check that you have everyone who signed in.

Having your opening, middle, and end planned for older students will keep your library running smoothly so you can focus on what is really important—working with students and teachers so they become efficient users and producers of information and ideas.

KEY IDEAS

- » Managing a classroom is not the same as managing a library.
- » You must always be conveying that the library is a safe, welcoming environment.
- » For librarians on a fixed schedule, the students "dropped off" by teachers are not theirs, but the classroom teachers'.
- » The physical setup of the library is very different from a classroom, and its open environment is a temptation for students to go a little wild, particularly if their teacher is not present.
- » Volunteers also judge how you deal with students and will spread the word, good or bad.
- » Today's students are not better or worse from the past, just different.
- » Most students have been born in the twenty-first century. Many historical events recent to us are ancient history to them.
- » What we consider technological marvels have always been present for them.
- » Control comes from fear and insecurity.
- » Management comes from confidence, acceptance, and tolerance.
- » Uncertain teachers and librarians try to control; great teachers manage.
- » Most communication is nonverbal.

» A negative attitude about an incoming class will be communicated in your body language and your tone of voice.
» Without change, there is no change.
» Students and adults live up—or down— to your expectations.
» To change your attitude, change your thinking.
» Effective classroom management can easily be achieved by having positive rules and established routines.
» To create a warm, welcoming environment, library rules should emphasize positives rather than negatives.
» For each lesson, know how you will manage the opening, middle, and end, so students can transition seamlessly from one to the other.
» Be prepared to handle students who are disruptive on arrival.
» The middle section, which is the heart of the lesson, should conclude with a discussion of the "essential question."
» You need an effective routine to bring a class to an end and transition the students out of the library.
» Exit tickets are an excellent technique to bring the lesson to a complete end and are an effective way for students to recall the key points of the lesson.

Notes

1. Beloit College. Mindset 2019. https://www.beloit.edu/mindset/2019.
2. Thompson, Jeff. "Is Non-/verbal Communication a Numbers Game?" *Psychology Today*. https://www.psychologytoday.com/blog/beyond-words/201109/is-nonverbal-communication-numbers-game.

BECOMING AN EXPERT TEACHER

You have numerous duties, roles, and responsibilities. As a reminder, in *Empowering Learners: Guidelines for School Library Programs,* AASL identifies four roles: teacher, information specialists, instructional partner, and program administrator.[1] Each has several responsibilities, but of those four, you will only be evaluated and judged by the first.

Your principal or supervisor observes you teaching a whole class. Although your job description includes a number of other roles, the sole method of assessing how you do your job is your teaching. Middle- and high-school teachers who bring their classes to the library for instruction will judge you based on how well you teach. If they don't think you do so well, they won't trust you with their students. At the elementary level, your volunteers will watch how you teach and rate you based on that.

Few within the educational community stop to realize that, just as with managing the library, teaching within the library setting is not the same as teaching in a classroom. Even those who were classroom teachers before they became school librarians can find the adjustment difficult. For librarians who were not originally teachers, it can be even more difficult.

THE CHALLENGE—PART 2

You now have techniques for ensuring that you expertly manage the library environment. However, you must also become a great teacher. Teachers can vary in their quality. Some are better than others, but for you to be regarded as a leader, you must be an outstanding teacher—one who knows how to involve and motivate students. More than that, your teaching needs to reinforce your mission, vision, and philosophy for your library program. Which means you must always create a welcoming, safe environment where people enjoy being.

Those at the middle- or high-school level with a flexible schedule have it marginally better. The teacher comes along with the students. If you planned the period in collaboration with the teacher, it tends to go well. The assignment will be graded, even if you aren't the one administering it. The teacher is there, overseeing the kids. Of course, you are being observed and judged by the teacher, which can be intimidating until you have established your reputation.

At other times, the teacher hasn't worked with you but has given the kids an assignment in which you are not expected to participate. All that's needed is the use of the library computers. The students immediately go to Google or Wikipedia, if your school allows access to it. Your databases are ignored as students race to a quick answer without knowing anything about creating a search strategy.

Worse, under these circumstances, it is likely the entire assignment requires merely an accumulation of easily found facts. The teacher doesn't recognize that locating the capital of a country and/or its current leader does not develop critical thinking skills, the understanding of what constitutes inquiry-based research, or students' ability to use their findings to create new knowledge—all skills necessary for their success in college and beyond.

In this situation, you need to use all your diplomatic skills. See if the teacher will give you a copy of the assignment. Consider ways it could be expanded so that students use the facts to do something. What databases do you have that might work with the research? Then quietly go over to the teacher and say that you know the assignment has already been set, but next time you would love to help him or her to cause students to go further.

Discuss the possibilities you envisioned. Let the teacher know that if he or she sends you a copy of the next research project before it is given to students, you will see how the library resources can be used to make it a more rigorous assignment. Rigor is always a good word. It was in Common Core and is likely to find its way into ESSA.

Let the teacher know that you will teach students how to access the information now needed for the project. If the teacher is at all interested, you have taken the first step to future collaborations, where you will have to demonstrate your qualities as a teacher. Don't be upset if the teacher doesn't follow up. Just keep repeating your offer when the class returns for the next assignment.

Another flexible schedule scenario is the teacher who, once the students are in the library, ignores them completely. Those teachers will read a newspaper or magazine, or go into your office and check their cell phones. The kids are well aware their teacher is MIA and will act accordingly. As the noise level increases and some students wander into the stacks, you need to take charge. But don't do so without getting the teacher's approval or you may be criticized.

Locate the teacher and ask if it's all right if you get the kids to "settle down" or would he or she prefer to do it. If you are given permission, don't yell at the kids. That only adds to the noise level. Go over to them and let them know they need to get back to work, and if they need any help, you will be glad to work with them.

Once you recognize the challenges, you can be ready to deal with them. The more times you do so successfully, the better you will get at it. If it doesn't work, figure out what you could have done differently and learn from it.

ANTICIPATE

New librarians spend a lot of time writing lesson plans if they are required. If you are more experienced, you tend to go through the process almost on autopilot. You know what you are doing. You have done it before. Plug everything into the required template. You are good to go.

If you are working with a teacher at the middle- or high-school level, you discuss the project. You know what you are teaching. You know the resources. Perhaps you pull some print resources off the shelf, and check the databases and any other online resources you want to use for the lesson. Perhaps you create a webliography, pathfinder, or some other tool to aid students on to the next task.

While that may work in the classroom (although it isn't the best way), it rarely works in the library. In planning, you determined what *you* would do, but you didn't anticipate student reactions. Old-fashioned teaching consisted of a teacher in front of the classroom, lecturing or giving directions while students followed them. It was rote learning, and frankly, little stuck in students' heads unless it was endlessly drilled.

Learning involves you *and* the students. In your planning, you need to think about what students will do with what you are saying and doing. What do they already know that will be useful? Do you need to help them remember those things? Where might they run into difficulties? What can you do to mitigate those?

You have discovered methods for managing the library environment, including routines and good transitions, but if a lesson is poorly conceived and/or doesn't anticipate problems student might encounter, it often results in discipline problems. When students flounder, they don't usually ask questions—unless you have set up a climate that expects that. What they tend to do is tune out. The slower students decide that once again they are "too stupid" to be able to do this—so why bother? As an increasing number of students stop working and find other "amusements," you lose control of the class because you haven't managed the situation.

I once observed an extreme situation. I was in charge of the K–12 librarians in a district. Although I didn't evaluate them, I was expected to lead them. A principal asked me to see what kept an elementary librarian from managing her classes well. I arrived at the library just before the last period of the day. Her plan was to read a story to the first graders that were coming in and then discuss it.

She decided to read Hans Christian Andersen's *The Emperor's New Clothes.* The students sat on a rug while she read the book and showed pictures, but the class soon became restless, shifting a bit and looking at the displays nearby. The librarian was so focused on the book, she didn't notice the children's behavior. When she began asking questions at the end of the story, the kids were unable to answer. She restated the questions, but they had no clue what she wanted.

What went wrong? It began well before she started. She had failed to anticipate and her preparation was seriously flawed. The first thing she failed to realize was that, by the end of the day, first graders have trouble focusing. They don't have that long of an attention span.

The next problem involves the librarian's decision to choose the story at the last minute, without spending any time going over it. Had she given it some thought, she would have realized that not only was the story too long, but it was filled with words many of the students didn't know. Among them were: swindlers, exceedingly, attendants, loom, procession, courtiers, and chamberlains. On almost every page, there was at least one word that most first graders couldn't understand. Even if they had the vocabulary, the story's moral was far too difficult for them to comprehend from the plot.

It would have been far better to read three very short stories on the same theme. Then she could have asked students to compare and contrast the stories and explain why one of them was their favorite. You need to set students up for success. When they know classes with you make them feel good about themselves, they will behave much better. So, not only will they learn more, but you also will have fewer discipline issues.

Anticipating when students might have problems or difficulties minimizes the chance that they will disengage from a lesson. Provide scaffolding as needed. It might be having a vocabulary sheet prepared, or better yet, having the students work in pairs to find out the meaning of words and terms they will be encountering while doing the research. For lower grades, prepare to pause during the story, reading first what it says and then restating it with the definition of the word.

Many librarians open a research project by having students sit at tables, and then giving them directions and telling them where they can find resources. If you look closely, you will see students who are not listening. They want to get started, and Google is waiting. Instead of *telling*, *ask* them how they plan to begin. You can offer one or two suggestions, but let them go quickly.

Another way to deal with a research project is to let students get started immediately and have them come back in about 10 to 15 minutes to discuss what is working and what isn't. If they think their Google search gave them what they needed, ask further questions to guide them into realizing where they have fallen short. Then let them know you have an easier way. Now they will be ready to listen.

Think about the gaps in students' knowledge that could be a barrier to their learning. At the high-school level, this might be looking at a work of literature they are about to study and recognizing that they need to know more about the time in which it was written and where it was set. English classes routinely do research on Elizabethan England before tackling Shakespeare, but the concept is not generally applied to other authors.

I once had a ninth-grade class assigned to read Alexander Solzhenitsyn's *One Day in the Life of Ivan Denisovich*. The book had been a best seller and wasn't particularly long, but students were struggling. The teacher asked if I could help, and I pointed out that the class was unaware of the weather and geography of Siberia, the way those deemed opposed to the government were treated, and the way the prison system in the U.S.S.R worked. We created a brief research project, giving them the opportunity to discover the harsh realities of Ivan Denisovich's world and why, by the end of the book, he felt it had been a good day—and what that said of his daily life.

ESSENTIAL QUESTIONS/ENDURING UNDERSTANDINGS

Whether or not you have to submit lesson plans, don't do your lessons "on the fly." I have known a number of elementary librarians who grab some picture books to read just before a class comes in, as did the one who read *The Emperor's New Clothes*. They know their collection and the stories within it, but when they select stories *this* way, they haven't given any thought into the deeper thinking they want students to do. Middle- and high-school librarians sometimes think it's sufficient to simply tell students which databases will be the most helpful in completing their assignment.

You are a teacher. It's one of your important roles. It doesn't serve you to be slipshod in your approach, no matter how busy you are. Students are your first priority. You want to give them your best, and your best is developing their critical-thinking ability from the earliest grades. The way you do it is with "essential questions" that lead to "enduring understandings."

An essential question should in some way address the reason why students are being asked to explore the topic. It's not about a specific skill ("Where do you find the call number on a record?" "How do you cite a book?"). It is not just facts ("What do you call a person who writes a book?" "Who were the Allies in World War II?"), nor does it deal with simple concepts ("How are fiction books arranged?" "Why or when should you choose a database over Google?").

"Essential" means of utmost importance or indispensable, and an essential question pushes students to think critically to probe for deeper meaning. It can and often should lead to further questions, setting the stage for lifelong learning. The more students are challenged by these questions, the better they will become at devising their own, which gets them beyond the surface understanding they so often have of a subject. For example, if they are reading Suzanne Collins' *Hunger Games* trilogy, essential questions might include: "What games besides the obvious one are in the series?" "How many types of hunger are incorporated into the trilogy?" "What would be another good title for the series?"

The concept of dealing with essential questions can start in kindergarten. There should always be a good reason at the heart of every lesson as to why it's important. The way you structure the lesson and the guiding questions you ask can get students to learn to think in more complex, critical ways. Some essential questions at the elementary level could be: "What do the illustrations add to the story?" "What differences, if any, are there when the illustrator and the author are the same person?" "What makes a good story?"

In essence, there are no right answers to an essential question, and the answer for any one can change over time. How you view a literary work when you are in your teens is quite different from how you might see it when you are in your thirties or fifties. The best essential questions recur throughout one's education ("How has this book/film/project changed my thinking/understanding/perception?").

Many librarians have been wrestling with a new professional essential question: "Is Dewey or a generified classification system the best for my students?" While this sounds like a yes or no question, there are so many layers and possibilities that it is core to what you do, and so it is definitely essential. Another ongoing professional essential question is, "When, if ever, is it justified to censor a book?"

When trying to figure out the essential question for a lesson or unit, ask yourself the following:

» Why is this being studied?
» What couldn't be done if we didn't understand this?
» How can it be applied to the larger world?
» What's worth remembering after this topic is finished?

The last question becomes the enduring understanding—what students take away from the lesson or project. Often, but not always, the enduring understanding is the individual's answer to the essential question. It speaks to the "big idea."

Enduring understandings are not truisms ("Celsius and Fahrenheit are two methods of measuring temperature."). They are not vague ("Google is not the only source for answers"), and they don't use adjectives ("Databases are very helpful in research."). The more essential questions and enduring understandings you create, the better you will become at creating them.

Like an essential question, an enduring understanding recurs throughout one's life. You make a connection from it to something new, and you have a deeper understanding of its importance and connection to core concepts. When you start your lesson planning with essential questions and enduring understandings, you give purpose and meaning to your teaching—and it will build your reputation as a teacher.

CREATING A CLIMATE FOR QUESTIONS

Lifelong learners don't have answers. They have questions to which they seek answers. What they find often leads to more questions.

The high-stakes testing that became central to the Common Core curriculum made our schools heavily focused on ensuring that students know the answers. It is what testing is all about. And tests produce the data, which in turn drives education. Although the new ESSA seeks to reduce testing, it isn't likely to disappear. Too much money is involved in testing.

The idea behind Common Core was that, by developing a more rigorous curriculum, students would improve their college and career readiness skills. The theory is that, with students better prepared for college and the work world, they will be better capable of competing in the twenty-first century. Even without Common Core and/or ESSA, classrooms have always focused on tests and answers. But the concept is seriously flawed.

Every teacher has experienced that frustrating student query, "Will this be on the test?" The subtext of which is, "If it isn't on the test, I don't have to pay attention." But answers merely show that students have demonstrated they have mastered the material as presented. They understand what has already been done—it's been achieved. It doesn't move them forward.

Answers end the discussion. You have the correct answer, we can now move on. By contrast, innovation is powered by questions. For true success, students must become innovators, posers of questions, and seekers of new solutions. Inquiry-based learning, which is at the heart of the *AASL Standards for the 21st-Century Learner* requires students to develop questions to direct their research into areas of interest to them around a given topic.

In many districts today, teachers are expected to formulate essential questions for units and lessons, and now you are able to develop quality ones for your library lessons. Many colleges want students to have an essential question rather than a thesis argument for their research projects. And yet, in the classroom, it's the answers that count.

Creating a climate for questioning opens students' minds to possibilities. It takes practice for you to come up with these questions, and students will also struggle in the beginning. They have come to identify success with the ability to answer questions, but ultimately, you want them to generate them.

To create the environment, avoid all questions with one-word answers. As with essential questions, it's best if there isn't one right answer. You can begin by asking for factual information. but then move quickly to deeper, more thoughtful ones.

At all grade levels, you can get thinking started by asking "What if?" and adding whatever relates to the topic at hand. For example, at the elementary level, after reading a story about summer or a sunny day, you can ask, "What if the sun shone every day?"

The first responses are apt to brush the surface of the issue. "I could go outside and play every day." Allow a few of those and follow up with, "What problems might result if the sun shone every day?" Now you will begin to get more thoughtful answers. Keep asking, "Anything else?" until they really begin considering the implications.

At upper grades, "What if?" questions can range from "What if we run out of safe drinking water?" to "What if Shakespeare were alive today?" The purpose is to get students thinking out of the box and consider implications, alternatives, and possibilities.

A question with a one-word answer can begin responses, but follow up immediately to have students probe the reasoning behind their answer. For example, I read *The Fisherman and His Wife* to a second-grade class. At the conclusion, I asked, "Who was responsible for the two of them remaining in their hut?" Hands flew in the air, and the response was "the wife." That is the one most would give since she kept wanting more. I asked the student why he thought she was the one responsible, and he responded in the expected manner.

I then asked, "Does anyone have a different answer?" A few hands went up, and a girl said, "The husband, because he knew it was wrong to keep asking for more, but he did it anyway." That opened the discussion to why someone does something they know is wrong and what they should do instead.

To be sure we had explored all possibilities, I again asked if someone had another answer. One boy raised his hand and said it was the fish. I assumed he said that since the fish was the only character left, but he surprised me. His reason was that the fish knew what would happen and kept leading the couple on. That went far deeper than I anticipated, and it set the stage for students to analyze other stories more deeply.

Always build in "wait time." Students have become accustomed to answering rapidly as though they were on a quiz show. Thoughtful answers don't come from the top of your head. Those who hold back the longest may have the best responses. Don't let them become overwhelmed and silenced by those who love to dominate discussions.

Make specific comments on their answers. Refer to an explicit idea they had or how they recognized something that wasn't obvious. By demonstrating you value their thinking processes, you create a climate for questioning.

Once students have become accustomed to your open-ended, thought-provoking questions, help them learn how to create them. Have them work in groups of two or three, and create three to five of these types of questions, related to what has been under discussion and/or any questions they might have about the topic.

Again, make positive comments about what they have come up with. Have students react to each other's questions. What answers do their classmates have to those questions? The more practice they have in doing this, the sooner you will be able to ask, "Does anyone have a question that will open up this topic in a new way?" Then, your students will be ready.

Long term, this means they will read and research with an open mind. They will be able to think, "What doesn't exist but would be great to have?" In other words, they will be the innovators they need to be to ensure their own success and to power the country.

ASSESSING

Good teachers know assessment starts before the lesson. There is no sense teaching something students already know. You will lose them before you begin.

Before designing the lesson, check with the teacher to find out what students have learned about the topic and what they still need to know. KWL charts are good not only for you but for the students. By recording what they already *know* and what they *want* to know, and then what they have *learned,* students are focused from the beginning and can see at the end what they have accomplished.

Throughout the lesson, keep assessing where students are. Is everyone following along? Who is not understanding the assignment or what they are doing?

Feedback should be almost constant. With elementary and middle grades, you can have them do a thumb's up, thumb's across, or a thumb's down, to let you know they "got it," are still working on it, or are completely confused.

Never ask, "Does everyone understand?" You will get head nods even from those who are clueless. No one wants to admit being lost. Instead say something like, "What hasn't been clearly explained so far?" You can also have a student summarize what has been done or said, and then ask if anyone has something to add to it. From their responses, you will have a good idea of where students are.

Watching students' faces is a sure clue as to whether they are engaged or have lost the thread of what they are supposed to be doing. With a complex project, you can have them list two things a student might misunderstand about the assignment. Graphic organizers are particularly good for visual learners to show what they are learning or doing. By checking on them while they are working you can assess where students are.

When storytelling ask questions a few times during your reading. Make sure students understand the vocabulary. For example, if you were to read *The Emperor's New Clothes*, ask students what they know about tailors. Also, see if students are following along with the story well enough to predict what might happen.

Summative assessments at the end of a lesson or unit are often quizzes or tests. Rather than do that in the library, have students look back at their KWL charts and share what they put in the third column. Exit tickets, discussed earlier, can also provide a summative assessment.

End products created by students frequently serve as assessments, but you can do even better than that. A culminating discussion in which students comment on the different presentations gives a fuller picture. Finishing up by having students respond to the Essential Question(s) and sharing their Enduring Understandings will give you the best picture of what they truly learned.

COLLABORATE OR COOPERATE

Many librarians have struggled with getting teachers to work with them but you will never be regarded as a leader if you work alone in your library. From the teachers' perspective, they have no reason to cooperate or collaborate with you. Things have been working fine so far. The demands being placed on them by Common Core (or whatever ESSA brings) means they are too tired to add anything to their workload or to take time away from the driving imperative to get through the required curriculum.

Despite these facts of education life, you must be able to work with teachers in some way. The workload must be all on your shoulders. The teachers must feel you have eased their burden, not added to it. As a bonus, you should also make them look good.

At the elementary level and a fixed schedule, the best you can hope for is to have cooperative units. This means you work separately toward a common goal. Reach out to teachers in grades four to six with whom you have a friendship. Ask about an upcoming unit of study and say you would like to have their students do work that complements it when they come for their library period. You should get a positive response from at least one teacher. If teachers can't or won't cooperate, at least try to get them to coordinate with what is going on in the classroom.

Using what you have learned about Essential Questions and Enduring Understandings, develop a mini-research project. It needs to be completed in one or two periods or it will have stretched out too long. You will want students to work in groups and utilize both print and online material. Select an appropriate presentation resource or app. While tech should never be the focus, you want to demonstrate how to integrate it into the curriculum, as well as show your own tech expertise. When the teacher sees it, you will have motivated him or her to try it as well. You can add that you will explain how teachers can use it when they are working with their class on something not connected with the library.

The students should use information ethically (appropriately citing print and digital sources) and have lots of visuals in their work so you can display it on your website. Indicate that the project was done in cooperation with the teacher to further explore the unit students were studying in class. Not only will this showcase the library program, it also puts the teacher in the limelight.

In middle and high schools, it should be easy to collaborate with teachers and work jointly on a unit, with each of you bringing your special area of expertise, but it doesn't always work that way. Some teachers seem to not think of the library in their planning. Other teachers bring their classes to the library but don't recognize you have a contribution to make.

Chapter 4 provided suggestions for how to slowly encourage teachers who bring their classes in to have you work with them. You can also start by talking to the teachers who are your friends. They still might be resistant, but if you gently keep offering, they will probably relent.

Even in the days before Common Core—and much of the technology we have today—I had to deal with teachers who felt they couldn't afford class time to bring students to the library for research. I finally convinced one science teacher to let me do a quick project with her students, using just one period instead of the typical three or four. At the end of the school year, she said she wanted to do more research projects with me. As a result of the one period in the library, her students did such better work that she felt the time in the library was well spent.

Ask to see the research being planned before the class comes to the library. If you don't see an essential question, suggest one or two to help frame the unit. Be open to changes from the teacher, and be sure students have the background to understand the project. Starting them off with a list of words and phrases to research can give them an understanding of terms they will use in their searches and provide a better grasp of the topic. The list can be divided up, and students can work in groups of two or three people. This gets them through the project more quickly, and they can share their findings with each other.

As with the elementary grades, select one or two web resources students can use to make their final presentations. You might choose Piktochart (https://piktochart.com), EasilLY (www.easel.ly), or anything else you have discovered to be helpful. The possibilities increase almost daily, so look for recommendations from your colleagues and AASL's Best Websites for Teaching and Learning (www .ala.org/aasl/standards/best/websites).

When the unit is complete, and you have shared student work—with credit to the teacher— discuss what worked, what would help the project next time, and any other changes the teacher thinks might be helpful. Ask questions that will bring honest answers, and be prepared for negative feedback. Don't say, "Did you like the way the project went?" as that will only give you a positive response that won't provide valuable feedback.. Instead say, "Was there anything you think could have been done better?" And make sure to let your administrator know about the project, again crediting the teacher.

INQUIRY-BASED LEARNING AND OTHER VARIATIONS

At all levels, your lessons should be developing students' critical thinking skills. Inquiry-based learning does just that and is at the heart of the *AASL Standards for the 21st-Century Learner.*[2] In essence, it requires students to develop questions relating to the topic and the essential questions. The purpose is for students to use prior knowledge to create new content and expand their understanding in a way that makes the new learning relevant to them and of value to others.

As noted earlier, being able to give the right answer does not prepare students to become contributors to our society or to become participants in a global culture. Invariably, inquiry-based learning requires students to work in groups with all members contributing their previous knowledge to better generate relevant questions. The group brainstorms together to determine a search strategy, organize their findings, and hopefully prepare a useful final product.

Students can use tech resources to keep track of what they are finding and doing, but that is not always necessary. For some classrooms, paper on tabletops or a whiteboard can help students graphically organize their project. This can be helpful in gaining control of a project that has many potential directions. By seeing the various pieces, the groups can identify the true focus. If necessary, they can take a picture of their visualization.

For the most part, the questions student create need to be open-ended and not fact based: "Who was the first president of the United States to do whatever?" The answers to open-ended questions will come from multiple sources, with the group weighing the validity and merit of each. At the youngest levels, it helps to have the class generate questions with two separate groups working on one of them. The groups can bring back their findings and conclusions and share with the class, engendering discussion. The class as a whole can then determine a logical organization and create a final presentation.

If you are not confident with designing an inquiry-based unit, search out examples online, or use your state's electronic discussion board or other means you have of connecting with colleagues. Ask for their favorite projects; it will give you ideas for developing your own.

The challenge as a librarian is to keep students on track. You need to monitor where they are in the process and be ready to help them when they hit a roadblock. This doesn't mean you tell them where they should go. By asking the group questions, you can guide them into getting past what has stopped them. It's important that the result be their own thinking, not simply finding what you want them to. That would be little different than asking "teacher questions" where you know the answer and students are expected to give it back to you.

Project-based learning presents students with a real problem. Depending on the curriculum and age of students, it can be anything from an environmental issue, such as clean drinking water when the supply is shrinking, creating a marketing program on healthy eating, to creating resources for others to use showing children's lives around the world. Similar to an essential question, each problem-based learning unit starts with an open-ended question.

The projects take time, so the unit can continue over several weeks or even a whole semester. The latter works best when it involves teachers across subject areas so that the curriculum requirements are infused throughout. Community service is often integral to the project. Technology is also usually a component, and as students are dealing with real world issues, they may connect with students around the world to obtain and share information.

In the process, students develop critical thinking skills, learn to collaborate with others, manage their learning process, and self assess. While everyone is to respond to the overarching question, much like with inquiry-based learning, students choose what they will work on, which increases engagement and leads to deeper learning. They learn to listen to others' ideas, receiving and giving feedback, and present their project to an audience wider than their classroom.

Problem-based learning is not simple, but it is effective. If you can find a teacher to work with you, it becomes a natural for showcasing the library program, although, as always, you will be putting the teacher and the students in the spotlight. Check programs of national and state library conferences to find ones that go into detail on creating problem-based learning projects.

Design-based learning is another less common variant. Students are challenged to design something useful. This technique has been used in college-level engineering classes as well as in entrepreneurial programs, but can be translated down to the elementary through high school students. Again, it should have an open-ended problem and/or an essential question.

The design-based project might pose the question of how to improve transportation on our nation's roads or how to make a better sneaker. The challenges frequently connect to STEM and/or makerspace programs. If at all possible, the completed projects should be displayed for the public to see and for community experts in the field to judge.

There are some variations in the thinking models for design-based learning but most include similar concepts. First, students must consider for whom they are designing the product and define what the end users' needs are. Next, they need to brainstorm without any limitations. The wilder the ideas the better, until they determine which of their ideas might work best. One or more prototypes might be constructed and tested to see what works and what doesn't. The answers fuel the next iteration of the idea.

Because the first prototype is unlikely to be fully successful, students need to develop persistence and be open to critique. Research is required at several steps along the way. And, of course, collaboration is an integral component.

You can see why all three of these approaches are considered twentieth-century learning approaches. To become lifelong learners, students need to recognize how much they can learn on their own, how to work with others, deal with challenges, and keep working until they are successful. The questions posed are their own, not the teachers' or the librarians.' With these approaches, students are interested, engaged, and invested in their learning. Their answers often lead to new questions, but the students are the ones choosing which questions to explore.

Although these approaches sound modern, at the turn of the last century, John Dewey was advocating learning by doing. It has taken more than one hundred years for education to catch up. Connect with your teachers to bring this way of learning into your library and your school. You will need to do most of the heavy lifting, but it's one more way to show you are a leader.

STANDARDS

All your teaching, no matter what approach you use, no matter how small the project, must be connected to standards. For years we worked with the Common Core Curricular Standards (CCCS). Now ESSA (Every Students Succeeds Act) is bringing new standards with it.

To be an expert teacher and a leader, you need to become very familiar with these standards and know how your lessons address them. More than that, you can help teachers cope with these latest changes by showing them how you are incorporating them. Successful librarians previously did that with CCSS and will do the same with ESSA. AASL has a "Crosswalk" with its standards and CCCS, and you can look for them to develop a new one for ESSA. Your state library association is working to keep you prepared as well. Know where to find these resources and use them.

In addition to the curricular standards, you should also address AASL's standards. These have been around since 2007 and will be updated in the fall of 2017. Once they are published, you need to stop using the older ones. Far too many librarians held on to *Information Power: Building Partnerships for Learning*[3] long after it was replaced by *Empowering Learners: Guidelines for School Library Media Programs*. We are leaders and innovators and must recognize that we need to change with the times.

ISTE (International Society for Technology in Education) recently updated its Standards for Students,[4] replacing the 2007 set. Standards for teachers and another for administrators will follow, along with standards for computer science educators and coaches. The changes between the old and the new are highly significant and highlight what has happened in the intervening nine years. The areas covered in the 2007 standards are:

- » Creativity and Innovation
- » Communication and Collaboration
- » Research and Information Fluency
- » Critical Thinking, Problem Solving, and Decision Making
- » Digital Citizenship
- » Technology Operations and Concepts

At first glance they seem quite appropriate for today's students—until you see the new areas which are:

- » Empowered Learner
- » Digital Citizen
- » Knowledge Constructor
- » Innovative Designer
- » Computational Thinker
- » Creative Communicator
- » Global Collaborator

Four indicators are given for each area. The standards are available as a free download. Show them to your administrator, and compare them with the previous ones. Discuss the implications of the changes and why the library program is perfectly positioned to help students achieve them.

KEY IDEAS

- » You will be judged by everyone on your teaching, despite the many other roles and tasks you have.
- » Teaching in the library is very different from teaching in the classroom.
- » For those on a flex schedule, the teacher will judge your effectiveness as a teacher by how you work with his or her class.
- » You need to slowly guide a teacher who brings in a class to do a facts-only assignment without asking for any input from you.
- » Some teachers ignore their class when in the library. If students get out of hand, you must diplomatically ask the teacher if you can be the one to restore order.
- » It's not enough to write a lesson plan, you need to anticipate how students will deal with the information you are presenting.
- » Consider students' age and experience along with the time of day.
- » Scaffold as needed to minimize obstacles that might cause students to stop working seriously.
- » Set students up to succeed.

» Begin planning a lesson/unit by determining its essential questions and enduring understandings.
» Essential questions do not have a single right answer and push students to develop critical thinking skills.
» From the earliest grades, students should be challenged with essential questions.
» Enduring understandings are the "take-aways" from the lesson/unit.
» Enduring understandings recur throughout life and often add a deeper, broader meaning to new learning.
» Answers are an end, only responding to what is already known.
» Questions open the mind to critical thinking and creating what isn't known.
» Innovation is powered by great questions, not good answers.
» Avoid questions with one-word answers.
» "What-if" questions open students' minds to possibilities and encourage them to expand their sense of wonder.
» After modeling questions, have students work in groups to create their own questions.
» Assessment is done before, during, and at the end of lessons.
» For a "needs" assessment, talk with the teacher and have students do a KWL chart.
» Thumb signals, graphic organizers, and reading students' faces work well for assessing how students are doing.
» For a summative assessment, use exit tickets, end products, and a culminating discussion including answering the essential question(s), and having students talk about their enduring understandings.
» At the elementary level, work to develop cooperative projects that complement what is being studied in class.
» Elementary cooperative projects need to be completed in one or two class periods in order to be aligned with the classroom unit.
» In reaching out to teachers, make it clear you won't be adding to their workload, as you will take care of it.
» Incorporate tech without having it drive the project.
» Review a middle- and high-school project, and suggest essential questions if none have been included; recommend one or two additional questions if needed.
» Share student work beyond the library, giving credit to the teacher.
» Let your administrator know about the teacher's project with you as well.
» Together assess what could make the unit better next time.
» Inquiry-based learning is inherent in the AASL Standards.
» In inquiry-based learning, students generate the questions they will research in order to build new content.
» Problem-based learning is similar to inquiry learning, starting with a real-world problem to which students must find a solution.
» Design-based learning challenges students to design a better alternative to something.

» All three approaches promote asking meaningful questions, hands-on learning, collaboration, research, and deeper learning.
» Because learning and projects in all three approaches stem from students' personal interests, they are interested, engaged, and involved in their learning.
» Become familiar with ESSA requirements and incorporate them into your teaching.
» Help teachers do so as well.
» Start using the new AASL standards as soon as they are published.
» Download the 2016 ISTE *Standards for Students*, and connect your teaching to them as well.
» Discuss with your administrator the implications of the changes in the ISTE standards from those published in 2007.

Notes

1. American Association of School Librarians. *Empowering Learners: Guidelines for School Library Programs.* (Chicago: American Library Association, 2009), 16.
2. American Association of School Librarians. *AASL Standards for the 21st-Century Learner.* (Chicago: American Library Association, 2007), www.ala.org/aasl/sites/ala.org.aasl/files/content/guidelines andstandards/learningstandards/AASL_Learning_Standards_2007.pdf.
3. American Library Association and Association for Educational Communications and Technology *Information Power: Building Partnerships for Learning.* (Chicago: American Library Association, 1998).
4. ISTE. Standards for Students. (Arlington, VA: ISTE, 2016). www.iste.org/standards/standards/for -students-2016.

PART II

BUILDING YOUR
LEADERSHIP SKILLS

You are now ready to take first steps on the path to becoming a leader. Reviewing your accomplishments so far should help build your confidence. Each time you move a bit further out of your comfort zone, you should recognize not only did nothing terrible happen, but you also become aware that being a leader is intrinsically rewarding. It makes you feel good about yourself to realize that as a leader you are important to the success of others. Your mission becomes apparent to a greater number of your stakeholders, and you bring your vision that much closer to reality.

In Chapter 5 you will take the first real steps in becoming a leader. You will discover how to build your confidence, and find mentors and role models (and the difference between the two). Suggestions for some low-risk projects show you how to build your reputation as a leader and reinforce the confidence you are developing.

Chapter 6 reveals you have more strengths than you realize. Start by discovering the Five Bases of Power. You may think you have little or no power, but in reality all bases are available to you. Two types of power not only helpful but you can use them easily once you are aware of them.

Discover the importance of building relationships. Becoming proficient in this area will lead to or improve collaborations with teachers and help you achieve the recognition you have been looking for from your administration. You already started working on that when you learned to be a team player. Related to knowing how to build relationships is discovering why being likeable is a quiet way to extend your leadership. You have addressed this in part by seeing a sense of humor as a leadership quality.

In Chapter 7 you improve your expertise as a leader. You may have been concerned originally as to how you could fit leadership into your already tight schedule. Learn techniques of time management that will work for you. Explore emotional intelligence (EI) to identify which components you have and which ones you need to develop further. Being able to draw on your EI helps you handle challenging people and situations.

The terms *leading* and *managing* are often blurred, but there are real differences between the two. You need to know how to do both and when to use each. It helps if you can identify which one you are doing at a given time.

Meetings often cause negative reactions. Too often, teachers and others see it as a waste of their valuable time. The more leadership roles you take on, the greater the likelihood that you will be leading a meeting. How can you mitigate any resistance? What should you do to make teachers feel their time is well spent?

As your presence becomes larger and your responsibilities increase, Chapter 8 helps you identify subtleties in getting your message out. Communication is an important component of leadership, and with so many platforms and methods of communicating, it is imperative that you recognize which one to use when and with whom. Developing your communication skills is critical to your eventual success.

Being perceived as a leader and expert, you will be called on to give presentations. By starting small and with a friendly audience, you can develop and polish your skills that will help you look professional and have impact. Learn to watch out for the unintended messages you send, and build relationships with the often-challenging technology department.

Pause as you finish this part. Reflect on how far you have come. Leadership is no longer an unachievable goal. You are being recognized as a leader by others. Congratulate yourself.

CHAPTER FIVE

BECOMING A LEADER

↗ You are well on your way in your leadership journey. You made the first step by recognizing that becoming a leader is not an option and accepted the challenge. You have honestly confronted some of your roadblocks, and identified qualities of leadership—some of which you have and others you will need to work on.

With a mission and vision, you have claimed your "space," proclaiming how you and your program are unique within the school and what you are aiming to achieve. Honing your skills as a teacher, you proved your worth to those who defined you solely by that role. Now it is time to take a few more steps, emerge from the library, and begin your role as a leader.

DEVELOPING CONFIDENCE

No one follows someone who is unsure of herself or who second-guesses her every move. If you are just starting out as a leader, it is hard to feel confident. To some extent, it's a case of "fake it till you make it," but you don't want to make any serious missteps this early in the process.

One way to help you "fake it" is to dress as though you are a leader. (You really are, but you need to convince yourself.) Comfortable clothes that let you sit on the floor if you are an elementary librarian or move around your library without feeling constricted is not the same thing as not paying attention to how you are dressed. Look professional—and confident.

Every elementary educator knows that on "picture day" when students come to school all dressed up, their behavior is better. Would high school proms be so special if they didn't require formal wear? When you dine at a fine restaurant, you choose your clothes with care. Our clothing reflects how we feel about something, and as a corollary, we react based on the way we are dressed. More on the role dress plays is provided in Chapter 11.

Confident people are optimistic. If you are a pessimist it's almost impossible to feel confident about anything. You can always see how it can go wrong and why it can't work. Cultivate an optimistic outlook on life, your job, and what is happening in education.

The naysayers are all around you, and sometimes it is easy to get sucked into negative thinking and speaking. The stresses in education, along with the seemingly widespread view that teachers are lazy and not doing a good job, make it difficult to find positives. You need to take the same approach you did with those challenging classes. By changing your attitude, you change your perspective.

One way to look at it is to recognize that when things are going smoothly, few people ever try to do anything differently. However, if times get tough, people need more help. As a librarian, you are in a position to aid harried teachers, if you are prepared to do so.

Many librarians felt left out by Common Core. The successful ones saw how stressed teachers were with the standards and benchmarks and showed teachers they could lift some of the burden by dealing with many of the anchor standards. With Common Core being phased out and ESSA on the way in, librarians have a new opportunity. Not only does ESSA recognize librarians and what they do, it also will be putting a whole new set of requirements into place. Teachers and administrators are concerned about what the future holds.

Stay on top of the changes as they occur. With help from AASL and your state library association, you will be among the first to understand the implications and what needs to be done. You can then confidently help your teachers navigate the new waters.

When you had a challenging class or a teacher coming to the library, you recognized that changing your attitude and expectation of how terrible it was going to be, affected the way you reacted to them. Making a shift from pessimism to optimism can be managed the same way and bring similar results.

If you like affirmations, use them; otherwise, begin each day with any positive thought. Remember what you like about being a librarian instead of what is taking you away from that part of your job. Repeat your mission and vision statements, and think of one way you might move a step closer during the day. Remember your mission is your perspiration, but your vision is your inspiration and aspiration.

Positive thinking changes your body language and can affect your voice. No matter how much teachers complain, they really don't enjoy being around negative people. It sends them into a downward spiral and makes everything worse. Optimists are uplifting and you will find others respond to it.

One word of caution: you don't want to come off sounding like a Pollyanna. Wearing rose-colored glasses means you aren't seeing the real world. What a true optimist offers is how to deal positively with problem parents, difficult administrators, challenging students, and all the other stuff being handed down as though you and the teachers don't know how to do your jobs.

Surprisingly, you can be confident and still ask for help. In many ways, that builds your confidence since you are discovering if you are on the right track. Don't ask questions hesitantly, as though you are unsure. Instead, say something like, "I have a decision to make (or whatever it is) and I value your advice." Oddly enough, this makes the person you ask see you as a confident person, as people who aren't confident are usually too worried or uncertain to seek advice.

Learn to speak with confidence. You might think this is not simple, but there is an easy first step. Monitor how you end a sentence when expressing an idea. Does your voice go up as though you are asking a question? This speech pattern has become common particularly with women and girls. It implies you are uncertain about what you are saying.

Become familiar with educational and library issues. AASL's and your state association's web page report on these. They give background information. From there, you can pick up the language in use. Practice talking about these topics by looking into a mirror at home. When you can speak without too many pauses or needing time to recheck the information, you are ready to share your "expert" opinion on the issues. And you will sound confident.

The final way to project confidence is to smile. This doesn't mean you should paste one on your face and wear it throughout the day. Smile and mean it. Smiling and nodding as students, teachers, or guests speak to you communicates optimism and friendliness—both attributes of confident people.

IDENTIFYING AND USING ROLE MODELS AND MENTORS

Role models and mentors can help you find your best path to leadership. These people are all around you, but you must identify them. They are not likely to seek you out.

Eventually, you will develop an extensive professional and personal learning network (PLN). You will draw on these people throughout your career. The connections will deepen, and you, too, will become a role model and a mentor.

Role Models

In the early stages of becoming a leader, it is very helpful to seek out role models. You don't interact with them, so they never know you have chosen them. Become an observer. Your role model can be a teacher or an administrator.

Choose someone who is able to get things done almost effortlessly—a person most others admire and are willing to follow. Recognize that no one has universal support. Being a good leader and highly regarded can make some people jealous. The chronic complainers can always find fault. And sometimes, it's just a personality clash.

See how your role model dresses and whether he or she projects confidence. How do they do that? Do they smile? Do they get to the point quickly? Is what they are asking or suggesting clear?

Continue watching until you recognize the many ways they communicate their leadership. Keep a notebook to remind yourself how they show they are leaders. Note how they enroll people to be a part of whatever they are proposing.

Do they ask for help or advice? How do they phrase it? When they praise someone, is it a generic, "You always do so well," or is it specific and true? Note how people, including you, respond to their requests. What makes it easy to do so?

Don't overlook negative role models. They can teach you as much as positive ones. If you select a teacher, observe body language. Is it relaxed and welcoming, or is it tight? Does this person smile a lot or frown frequently?

Listen to the tone of voice. For your negative role model, you will probably find it a bit sharp and often judgmental. Are criticisms directed at a person or an idea? How often do you hear the person say thank you? Is this also reflected in how he or she interacts with students? Most often the same behaviors can be seen in all relationships.

Start a different notebook to record how negative messages are sent. It's very likely this person is unaware of what he or she is projecting. You want to be sure you don't have any of those characteristics.

Mentors

Having studied both positive and negative role models, it's time to consider a mentor. Unlike role models, you never select a negative mentor, and you do interact with them. Although you might ask your role model to become your mentor, it's not necessary.

If you choose a teacher in your building, do so carefully. Select someone who will be discreet since you don't want this relationship to be common knowledge as you will be asking how to handle some possibly difficult situations with colleagues or administrators. Additionally, a teacher might not understand all your roles or recognize the best way to translate it into leadership.

In general, a school librarian is likely to be your best choice. Think of the librarians you know in your state. Your mentor candidate need not be an officer in your state library association, but it should be someone who has proven to be a leader both in his or her building and in the library profession.

You can make the initial contact via e-mail and ask to set up a phone call to fully discuss why you want that person as your mentor. Almost anyone you select will be agreeable. On the phone call explain your job situation, the way you have been managing it so far, the way you think you are being perceived in the building by teachers and administrators, and why you want to become a leader. Also explain why you selected this person.

Ask your mentor how he or she wishes to proceed. Should further exchanges be done by e-mail or would a phone call be preferable? Should these be regularly scheduled or handled on an as-needed basis? It's up to the mentor to decide since you are the one asking for the favor. Of course, if you are faced with a sudden difficult situation, you should be free to reach out to your mentor even if it's not the scheduled time.

Whatever method you set up to maintain contact, always be on time. Your mentor is giving you a great gift, and you want to show you recognize it. Always follow your mentor's advice. You sought this person out because of his or her leadership abilities; you don't get to pick and choose which advice you will listen to. Let your mentor know what results you received from implementing their advice.

As you become more of a leader, you will not need your mentor as much. You may find that the relationship becomes more collegial as you share experiences. Hopefully you will have some opportunities to meet in person, perhaps at your state library association's conference. Your mentor will now be an important person in your PLN.

When you end the regular mentor/mentee contact, send your mentor a thank-you note to acknowledge all that he or she gave you. A gift is not required, but if you do give one, don't overdo it, and try to make it something that represents the relationship you shared. Someday in the future, you might be asked to be a mentor. That is how you really pay your mentor back for all the help you received.

TESTING YOUR LEADERSHIP SKILLS

It's time to try your leadership wings. Your first forays need to be no-risk. These ideas are almost guaranteed to succeed and don't require you to step far out of your comfort zone. Knowing you can't fail will keep you calm and allow you to discover how you bring your strengths as a librarian into leadership.

Your no-risk projects will begin letting others become more aware of your program and your value. Once you have begun to establish your reputation as something of a leader, you can propose one or more programs with limited risk.

No-Risk Ideas

Teachers are not nearly as familiar as you are with new Web and app resources that can be integrated into the classroom. Start sending out weekly e-mails promoting just one and explain how it might be used. For example, you might suggest *Make Beliefs Comix* (www.makebeliefscomix.com), which lets teachers and students easily create a three-panel comic strip. Possibilities for what can be done with it range from a simple book report that shows how well students can identify the main ideas, to an environmental message as part of a research project. Since the comic strips can be created in almost every language studied in school, world language teachers might be interested as well.

You also can mine the AASL Best Websites for Teaching and Learning (www .ala.org/aasl/standards/best/websites) and Best Apps for Teaching and Learning (www.ala.org/aasl/standards/best/apps). Try out some of them yourself and then send on the ones you like best to the teachers. Send the sites to your supervisor as well so administrators see that you are helping teachers integrate technology into learning.

Starting a book club for your students also has little to no risk. It does require some preplanning, and you should ask for approval from your supervisor. There are a number of different ways to run a book club, but considering your budget, it is probably best not to have everyone reading the same book.

Determine what time would work best in your schedule. Can kids come during lunch and eat in a special corner in the library? (That would be an incentive for many.) If not, you may have to hold it after school. Announce the formation of the club. Set up a display of titles in a wide variety of genres and have students pick one they want.

For the next and subsequent meetings, those who finished their book can share it with club members, talking about the positives and negatives. If they wish, have them write a review that can be included in the record on the OPAC, or start a section on your website "Recommended Books from Our Readers."

Search online for more ideas about running a school library book club. You may want to include other activities connected with students' reading. Whatever activities you choose should not make it sound like a school assignment but, rather, something fun.

In addition to this basic book club, another type of book club can be done with students in middle through high school. Students select a book of their choice and they and one of their parents read it. Once a month, the whole group gets together and discusses the different reactions the parent and the student have to the same book.

Not only does this intergenerational book club connect parents to the library, it also opens up some interesting dialogues between parents and children. In one case, a mother and her son read Hank Aaron's autobiography, *I Had a Hammer*. The mother had to discuss with her son why Aaron was so vilified. The talks at home became so interesting, and after feeling left out, the father also read the book.

Take videos of book club meetings and get members to talk about why they joined and what they like about the club. Include the video in your quarterly and/or annual report. If you haven't been doing these, you need to start, even if it isn't required. This is the best way to inform your administrator of what you do, and you want to keep the text to a minimum and spotlight student learning in these reports.

If you don't have one already, think about starting a "Battle of the Books" program in your school. It's more labor-intensive than the other two ideas, but it gets you working with teachers even if all of them don't have their students participate. The final competition is usually held in the evening, and you will want parent and/or teacher volunteers to help.

Get approval early from your principal, not only because of the evening competition, but also because you will need to find funding to purchase enough copies of the ten selected titles for students to read. Check your state library association's site to see if they have a section on Battle of the Books. Those that do list the titles for the year by grade level since some schools compete with each other. The books are usually available in paperback to keep costs down.

Low- to Medium-Risk Ideas

Gardening projects with elementary students bring multiple benefits. Planning the garden involves math skills, and teachers may cooperate with you on this. Funding is needed for the seeds and whatever will be used for harvesting. You might be able to get a local garden supply store in the area to donate the supplies and perhaps someone can come over and show students the best way to plant their different selections.

The project becomes even more rewarding if the vegetables grown are used by the cafeteria for student lunches, or better yet, donated to a local food bank or kitchen. Intersperse gardening chores with sharing books on growing the different vegetables and their nutritional value. Local media are often interested in filming the kids and interviewing them (with appropriate releases) about why they are creating the garden and how they feel about it.

Administrators are usually willing to approve this project because of its connection to STEM as well as showing how the school helps the community. The concern and emphasis on STEM makes them also amenable to an Hour of Code and Makerspace projects. Both of these are becoming more and more common in school libraries at every grade level.

Go to the Hour of Code website at https://hourofcode.com/us and learn more about this international movement that in one hour introduces coding to those "ages 4 to 104." The FAQs and a tab on how to promote the Hour of Code are very helpful and will answer just about every question you have, including: "Do I need a lot of computers and bandwidth?" and "What if I have no idea how to code?"

Although the Hour of Code officially occurs in December during Computer Science Education Week it can be done anytime. There are a number of different tutorials making it appropriate for all grade levels, ranging from "Code with Anna and Elsa" from the movie *Frozen*, to Minecraft activities. New tutorials are being created regularly and there is a link for how to continue to learn online. The Hour of Code can be a natural way to build interest in a Makerspace program for the library.

Information on Makerspaces abound on the Internet, but don't get inundated. You don't need a 3-D printer to get started, although they are a wonderful addition. You can start very small. Get advice—and a mentor—on this by asking for help on your state association's electronic discussion list.

Attend your state conference. There is nearly always a program on Makerspaces. The presenter, and possibly some of the attendees, can be excellent sources of help and advice. Go to #makerspace on Twitter and connect with the many librarians who are running Makerspaces. The pictures will inspire you.

Launch your Makerspace in very gradual steps. If you are at all crafty, start with what you know. See if there are any teachers who are good at various creative projects—from Legos to learning computing languages—and put their knowledge into practice. The Young Adult Services Association (YALSA) blog site http://yalsa.ala.org/blog/2015/10/14/looking-to-create-a-makerspace-in-your-library-here-are-some-ideas/ has some excellent suggestions for middle- through high-school projects.

Have a vision for your Makerspace. Why do you want to start one? What will kids learn from it? Consider the practicalities and logistics: When will you hold your Makerspace? How often? Do you want to do it as a club activity? Will everything be available at once or will you have different topics for your Makerspace with robotics at one session and creating home decorations at another?

Once you have an idea of what you want to include at the beginning, get approval from your administrator. Since you probably won't have funds until the program fully develops, you will need to get donations. Lego projects work at any grade level, as do K'nex. Kids and adults are often willing to send in materials they have at home. When you are more confident about running a Makerspace, you can raise money (again with approval) by going to a fundraiser site, such as www.donorschoose.org.

Plan for how and where you are going to store supplies and any tools you might need. How are you going to replace what is consumed? Can you get some funds from your parent teacher organization?

Don't forget safety. Establish rules for your Makerspace on how to use materials properly. Also include your expectations for cleaning up at the end. Depending on how many students are working, you may want to have at least one more adult in addition to yourself to keep an eye on students.

Get feedback from your students on which Makerspace activities they most enjoyed and what else they would like to see. When you are out and about, look at stores and shops that might be a source of help, such as a local hardware store or a knitting shop. See what the craft shops offer. Everything is a possibility if it is age appropriate and of interest to your students. The store owners might be willing to donate their time, expertise, and materials.

Any print materials you have about the Makerspace you are doing should be on display. They don't need to be direct resources, but they should give students information about the project. For example, if you are creating a Makerspace on robotics, any *current* books you have on robots might suggest possible things students can make in the future. Information about careers in the field can inspire kids as to how and where they might take their interest in the future.

You can download the *Makerspace Playbook* 2nd edition at http://makered.org/wp-content/uploads/2014/09/Makerspace-Playbook-Feb-2013.pdf. It is an 84-page manual with just about everything you need, but you might find it too much for when you are first starting out. Maker Ed has a *Youth Makerspace Playbook* http://makered.org/makerspaces, which can be downloaded for free or purchased in print.

Take pictures and videos of your Makerspace. Invite your administrators to view them. If you can bring in the media to cover the event, your principal, and possibly the superintendent, will show up as well. After the first year, review what worked, what didn't, and plan for how you will expand it the next year. You should get even more support, based on your success.

BEING A TEAM PLAYER

Leaders know how and when to follow. You might at first glance assume this means doing whatever the administration says. But legally everyone has to do that. If you refuse to follow a direct instruction, you are insubordinate, and in most organizations you can then be subject to termination.

Being a team player means you never sabotage or blindside administrators. You already know not to join in on any back-biting comments about your principal or supervisor. You don't have to defend them, but don't agree with the complainers. Someone always manages to let administrators know who is making negative statements. (Just don't be the one who curries favor that way.)

If a parent complains to you about how you treated her child or is upset about a book in the library, don't simply hope you have handled it and that the problem will go away. The last thing you want is for that parent to call the superintendent or a board member friend to air her grievances. You will not be the first one questioned. Instead, the board member will call the superintendent, who will call the principal. By the time you hear of it again, the situation has probably escalated, and you put your principal in a spot where he or she has to admit not knowing about something that happened in their building.

After you have spoken with the parent, contact the principal as soon as possible and explain the entire situation. Summarize what the parent said and how you responded. Whether your principal agrees with how you handled it or not, at least if the superintendent calls he or she is able to say they know what happened and the current status of the situation.

I once worked in a district where one board member liked to drop into the library, poke around, and ask questions. He was a difficult person as his agenda was to vote against anything that cost money. He had no children and seemed to think the school budget was generally a waste of taxpayer money.

I could never be sure whether he would bring up what he saw or what I said at a board meeting. To protect myself and my superintendent, I would call her as soon as this board member left, and report what transpired. That was being a team player, and it was much appreciated by my superintendent.

Team players know how to help. The library is often used for all kinds of meetings. Sometimes you are asked to close the library to accommodate the people coming in for a meeting, and other times you need to use a portion of your facility, which can possibly be screened off.

When asked to close the library, see if the administrator making the request is willing to have you close just a section. Point out you will have to cancel any class scheduled to come in at that time. If it's impossible, speak to the teacher and try to make it work by teaching the students the lesson in their classroom. It's easier if you have mobile computers or are a 1:1 school.

You aren't denying the administrator's request, which would be insubordination, nor are you being difficult, which would show you are not a team player. You are demonstrating that you are solution-oriented and you have an active program with teachers who collaborate with you. Insofar as it's possible, your supervisor will likely accommodate you.

Create a one-page fact sheet about your library program. Include items such as number of databases, total number of students who used the library last year and last month, and number of classes you worked with. You can even break it down by subject areas, particularly if you work with teachers in several departments.

Always have your fact sheet ready to go. Since an administrator may host meetings in the library during the school day, find out which group is coming and when. Print one copy of the fact sheet and ask the administrator if this would be useful to distribute. For example, if it's a realtors association or the Chamber of Commerce, this information shows how students are benefiting from an active program, and speaks to a high quality educational program, which is important to them.

For different groups, you may need to tweak your data a bit to show the parts of the program of most interest to a certain group. Administrators wouldn't know to ask for this information. By supplying it on your own, you show you are a team player.

How you handle administration requests defines whether you are a team player. At all levels, you may be asked to cover a class for a teacher when a substitute cannot be found. Your natural reaction might be to take issue with being treated as though you have less value than a classroom teacher. Since you must do what you are told, you have little to gain by complaining. It only will aggravate an already harried administrator.

In terms of requests to close the library, try negotiating. I was once asked to cover for a physical education teacher. I really didn't want to spend time in the gym. Rather than argue, I negotiated. I suggested instead of closing the library for the period, the students could be sent to the library, and I would work with them on a physical education mini-research project.

The department chair agreed, and I introduced students to a new database and pointed to ones they did and had them find information few people knew about a sport they loved. I showed them a way to present their information visually, and let them know I would be giving their work to their teacher. This ensured that they would stay focused and complete the task. In the process, students learned something new and the department chair came to value me as someone who could be trusted to work with him.

Turning what seems like an onerous job into something positive makes administrators realize how much they need you. I once completed a three-year renovation project of my library with the purpose of increasing floor and shelf space. I was extremely pleased with the results, but before I could enjoy the fruits of my labor, I was told I had to make room for the School to Career advisor.

Also at this time, central administration had to move into the high school for several years while the building was being repaired; everyone needed to make adjustments. The principal apologized but said he had no alternative. In addition, I had a large room that housed our back periodical collection. (This was in the early days of periodical databases, so we hadn't gotten rid of the old magazines yet.) This room would now house the Social Studies department.

I wasn't happy, but I knew my principal had no choice, and neither did I. I found one section that was not in the general flow of the room. I used some counter-height bookcases to help define the area and moved all our occupational material to those bookcases. I also worked with my clerk to get rid of all the magazines that weren't used for browsing and kept only the last year of those. What was left was housed in a room used by my clerk and where we also kept the books awaiting processing.

The results of this accommodation were all positive. The School to Career advisor was a skilled grant writer. He obtained computers and other tech equipment, which became part of the library inventory, and I didn't need to use my budget to purchase it. He also had funds to purchase manuals and books relating to his area, which were then included in the library's holdings. The social studies teachers found the proximity of their office to the library extremely helpful, and many collaborative projects grew out of this. And of course, the administrators appreciated all I had done.

Another way to show you are a team player is when professional development days are scheduled: offer to present a workshop. You can teach about databases that connect to certain subject areas. Use AASLs Best Apps for Teaching and Learning www.ala.org/aasl/standards/best/apps to introduce teachers to a variety of apps to use for STEM, organization and management, content creation, and different subjects. Use AASL's Best Websites for Teaching and Learning www .ala.org/aasl/standards/best/websites to show them websites for media sharing, digital storytelling, organization and management, social networking and communication, content resources, and curriculum collaboration.

Select several websites to highlight and give teachers an opportunity to explore them. Lead a discussion on different ways to integrate these into their classrooms. Let them know you are willing to work with them one-on-one to as they wish to develop proficiency with any of these sites. You have now made yourself and your program an instructional partner, shown the administration you are a technology integrationist, and as always, a team leader.

Look for occasions to serve on key committees. Volunteering is being a team player. The technology committee is a natural for you, but there might be others as well. Choose carefully. You want to be on a committee that gets things done.

Volunteer to help any group working on curriculum writing. If your district is doing curriculum mapping, you can also be of service. You will be plugging in library resources as the curriculum is being set, and teachers will naturally be working with you for those units.

None of these ways of being a team player require you to be a toady. At the core, you are demonstrating your value and expertise, and showing you are a leader and a source of help for all your colleagues.

IMPOSTER SYNDROME AND SELF-ASSESSMENT

You have taken the plunge and your offer to do a professional development workshop has been accepted. Instead of feeling elated, you are filled with doubts and begin second guessing yourself. This feels like much more than nerves when speaking before your colleagues.

The voices inside your head are saying you are not up to this challenge and you are not a skilled presenter. You have seen the polished job done by those at conferences or during professional development days in your school. What were you thinking? The teachers will wonder why you ever thought you could show them anything they needed.

Say "hello" to the "imposter syndrome." Described by Suzanne Imes and Pauline Rose Clance in the 1970s, it is increasingly being recognized for the widespread phenomenon it is.[1] High-achieving people internally question themselves and their value. They fear they aren't good enough. They tell themselves previous successes have been a matter of luck.

People who have won major awards deal with these feelings. Best-selling authors fear they aren't capable of writing the next book and it will be a flop. Most people have thought they were the only one dealing with these negative thoughts, but we are discovering it is far more prevalent than imagined.

Another manifestation of the imposter syndrome is the belief that you aren't worthy or special. The skills you have seem simple enough to you. Anyone can do them. Who would value the ability to do something that simple?

You see only what others do that you cannot. Perhaps you use Twitter in a limited way. So many librarians are leading Twitter chats and talking about how much they are learning on Twitter. So much for your tech ability. On Google+ someone posts a great unit they did with their students using a website or app you never heard of. How can you think you are a tech integrator when you don't know these things?

On the one hand, you know logically that no one is an expert in all aspects of librarianship or anything else. What makes the imposter thoughts so insidious is that they are coupled with the belief that your expertise is minor in the scheme of things and doesn't mean much. Someone I know once said, "Don't judge your inside by someone else's outside." You never stop to consider whether the person you think is so expert knows what you do.

Also, even though you are still on your journey to leadership and greater knowledge in your profession, that doesn't mean what you bring right now doesn't have value. Sometimes when you have a lot to learn, you are at the perfect place to introduce others to what you already know. Yet none of that matters when the imposter syndrome strikes.

On and on these negative thoughts spiral through your head every time you step out of your comfort zone. It makes you want to go back into your safe cocoon. When you are in that place, stop and remind yourself that the people you admire so much for their knowledge have the very same feelings and thoughts about themselves.

The bad news is no matter how competent and skilled you are, no matter how highly regarded you are, if you are prone to the imposter syndrome as so many are, these feelings will recur. The good news is you can easily deal with them. Once you know what triggers your reaction, all you need to tell yourself is that it's the imposter syndrome speaking to you. It's not the truth.

Now that you are aware of and are prepared to deal with the imposter syndrome, you are ready to do your first self-assessment of yourself as a librarian and leader. You have taken your first "safe" steps into leadership— the very first one in recognizing why it's important to be a leader.

You have analyzed and rejected the stories you have been telling yourself as to why you are not leader material, and identified a few important leadership qualities. Look back over them. Which ones do you possess? Tell yourself the truth. Integrity is bound to be one of them.

Do you have a sense of humor? Do you know how to put a positive spin on the various challenges confronting you and your teachers? Are you able to see the ridiculousness in some of what happens in the course of a school day and year? If so, that's another leadership attribute you have.

You probably still pause at the thought of being a risk taker. Moving into this area of leadership takes a bit more time. A self-assessment lets you see where you are succeeding and where you want to go next. While you might not see yourself as a visionary, you have created a vision statement for your library program that takes you beyond the more immediate focus of your mission statement. All the work you will be doing as a leader will help you on the path to realizing it.

How do you rate yourself as a classroom teacher? Which skills and abilities did you have before reading Chapter 3? Were there any areas you discovered where you want to improve? While improving is an important component of being recognized as a leader, you can work at improving all the time.

Have you been observing the role models you selected? Found a mentor? How far have you gotten in trying out a no-risk or low-risk project that will begin to show you are a leader?

If you are being honest with yourself, you are further along than you thought. You also are developing an understanding of where you want to go next. Always remember, leadership is not an option: It is a job requirement, and you are on your way there.

KEY IDEAS

» Leaders are confident. No one follows someone who is unsure and always second-guessing themselves.
» You can "fake it till you make it."
» Dressing with confidence means emulating the clothing choices of building leaders, whether they are teachers or administrators. Your attitude frequently mirrors how you are dressed.
» Develop an optimistic outlook and project it.
» Ask for help, but do so in a positive, rather than an uncertain, way.
» To sound confident when speaking, don't raise your voice at the end of a sentence, which implies you are asking a question rather than making a statement.
» Use your state and national associations to stay current with trends in librarianship and education, picking up the vocabulary so you can share the information confidently with others.
» Find a role model and observe how this person demonstrates leadership.
» Role models can be either positive or negative ones.

» You do not interact with your role model, nor let that person know you have selected him or her.
» The best choice for a mentor is a school librarian whom you identify as a leader in your state.
» Set up a procedure for communication with your mentor, based on your mentor's preference.
» Always be punctual for these contacts so as not to waste your mentor's valuable time.
» When the mentor/mentee relationship is complete, send a thank-you note acknowledging your mentor and how he or she helped you.
» Becoming a mentor in the future is how you return the gift to your mentor.
» Your first forays into leadership should be ones that are risk-free. From there you can build to low- and minimum-risk programs.
» Teachers can become aware of how you can help them if you send them regular messages about websites and apps to use in classroom projects.
» Student book clubs with kids becoming book reviewers are relatively easy to launch.
» Have students create a vegetable garden and give the produce to the cafeteria to use or donate to a local food bank or soup kitchen.
» Plan an Hour of Code.
» Institute a Makerspace, starting small and letting the program grow slowly to keep it manageable and successful.
» Get help and advice on Makerspaces from your colleagues, Twitter, and Internet resources.
» Always get administrator approval for any project you want to undertake.
» For all programs, take photos and make videos, invite the media and your administrators.
» Never blindside or sabotage your administrators. Inform them immediately of any potential issues that might cause problems.
» Be prepared with library data for administrators to use if needed when hosting a meeting with an outside group in your library.
» When faced with a request that doesn't support your program, negotiate to make it work in a more positive way.
» Offer to present a workshop on professional development days.
» Volunteer to serve on important committees.
» The imposter syndrome is the cause of the voices in your head saying you are not worthy, that others know more than you, and similar negative thoughts.
» The voices will always be there, but when you recognize it's not the truth but the imposter syndrome, you will be able to ignore them.
» Honest self-assessment, neither over- or understating your abilities and successes is necessary to get to where you want to go.

Note

1. Weir, Kirsten. "Feel Like a Fraud?" American Psychological Association. November 2013. www.apa.org/gradpsych/2013/11/fraud.aspx

CHAPTER SIX

UNCOVERING YOUR STRENGTHS

You have more strengths than you realize. It's time to discover what they are and how you can utilize them to build your leadership and make the educational community regard you as indispensable. The power is in your hands.

You explored some leadership qualities in Chapter 1. There are more to identify and once again evaluate the ones you already have and the ones you want to acquire. As a librarian you know knowledge is power. The more you learn about leadership, the easier it becomes to be a leader.

FIVE BASES OF POWER

Power carries many connotations, and people react differently to the thought of it. To some, it suggests authoritarianism, and it has often been that. In reality, power in itself is neutral. It is about the ability to influence people or things. How it is used determines whether it is positive or negative.

Those working in education assume only the administrators have power, and in some places, they feel the parents have all the power. But power resides in many hands. However, for it to have any purpose you need to understand the different types of power, as well as which ones to use and when.

In 1959, John R. P. French Jr. and Bertram Raven published a scholarly article, "The Bases of Social Power."[1] The business world has been using it for some time, and there are more accessible explanations of these five.[2] Starting with defining power as "the ability to influence others to believe, behave, or to value as those in power desire them to or to strengthen, validate, or confirm present beliefs, behaviors, or values," or in other words, to get someone to do what you want them to do, French and Raven identified these five types of power:

> » Legitimate
> » Coercive
> » Reward

» Expert
» Referent

Legitimate Power is what someone with a title has. The principal as head of the school has legitimate power. *Coercive Power* is the ability to punish someone if they don't do what you want. *Reward Power* is the opposite of coercive power. *Expert Power* is knowing something others need to know. *Referent Power* in layman's terms is charismatic power. People do what you want because it gives them an opportunity to work with you.

Anyone who works in a school knows if you don't do what the principal says, you are insubordinate, which can ultimately be cause for dismissal. Obviously, the principal has power to reward or punish by measures, such as your schedule and the students assigned to you. Being given a schedule that has a class of challenging students during the last period of the school day, year after year, is often a sign the principal is displeased with you.

While legitimate power is not something that can be argued, it is important to recognize that coercive and reward powers are both negative uses of power. If people are doing what you want only out of fear of some retribution, all you will get from them is the bare minimum. They won't do anything beyond what was strictly required. Reward power carries an inherent threat of being revoked if you fail to please. That causes second-guessing and mistrust.

Expert and referent powers are both positive uses of power. Often, expert power is of limited duration. People will follow the expert's directions until they also have mastered the skill or until it is no longer important to them. Referent power is long lasting. If you have the personality that engages others, they will always be willing and interested in working with you.

As a librarian, you technically have all five bases of power available to you. You have a title that makes you distinct from teachers, and you "rule" over the library. You can reward teachers by the above-and-beyond help you give them, or you can punish by not offering help if they don't realize what you can do for them. But as noted, these are not positive uses of power.

Your tech ability and your knowledge of searching techniques, new web resources, and apps give you expertise power. The more you share your knowledge, the wider the awareness of what you have to offer. This often results in teachers asking questions and for advice, and in many cases, collaborating with you.

It is of course your referent power that will serve you best. With morale low and stress high in most schools, if your library is an oasis of calm (not quiet), a place where positives are enjoyed and explored, and a relief from the constant judgment or assessment of teachers and students, people will be attracted to you. Throughout this chapter, you will find out more on how to build your referent power.

Power is not leadership, but there is a connection. Many of you have experienced principals who had legitimate power but were definitely not leaders. Having power doesn't make you a leader. However, knowing how and when to use it does.

Having a vision is an attribute of a leader, but if you are the only one holding it, whom are you leading? Developing a good idea and having the skills to execute it won't make you a leader if no one is joining in. You need to cultivate followers and you do it most often by using your power.

YOUR SKILL SET

The qualities of leadership are discussed on business sites and, to an increasing extent, on educational sites. What is most often overlooked is that these qualities must cause people to follow you. If you are marching forward and no one is following you, you are not leading—you are walking alone.

The first of your powers to cultivate is expertise. This is natural for you even if you haven't considered it before. Teachers know their subject matter. Administrators, hopefully, know how to ensure that everything in the building is going smoothly. But you have unique skills that no one else in the building has, many of which are needed by faculty, administrators, and students.

The Basics

You have more expertise than you know. Take stock of your "tool box" and see what your strong suits are and which are important for you to develop further. Don't overlook your background and hobbies. Some of you have come from professions outside of education. If you are from the business world, you can assess similarities and differences in how decisions are reached and how people interact. While you don't want to allude too often to how things are done in the corporate world, you can make use of this knowledge to see a better way to handle an issue.

Those of you who have an athletic background might be able to coach. This sounds like a reach from the library, but it can be extremely helpful to have people view you in a very different way. You get to work closely with students who you might not connect with otherwise, as well as faculty members who also are rarely seen in the library. Coaches are almost automatically seen as team players, so this is another way to present yourself.

Some of you are gamers. Others are skilled in various crafts. Don't dismiss these pursuits. As more and more libraries develop Makerspace programs, your hobbies are an excellent place to begin your offerings. It gives students and other teachers ideas for how they can become part of the program.

Your tech know-how is extensive and is something your colleagues need to learn. Even computer teachers don't have your broad knowledge of programs, searching techniques, web resources, apps, and more. They are focused on teaching specific programs to students. You bring far more. And you share your knowledge with teachers and administrators, as well as students.

At the elementary level, you, the special teachers, and the administrators see the big picture since you usually see all the students over the years, helping them learn and grow. At middle and high school, depending on how active a program you develop, you work with most students every year from the beginning orientation session to the more complex research projects they explore as they approach graduation. You can assess their growth along the way and, because you are a constant and have created a safe, welcoming environment, you support them through challenging periods in their life.

Unlike anyone else in the building, you have access to vast resources. The visible print library is the very tip of the iceberg. Many school libraries are connected to their state's interlibrary loan system. When your own collection doesn't have something, you can get it delivered to your library.

Your online materials multiply by many times what is available in print. More than that, if you belong to professional associations, you have connections to librarians in your state and at the national level who can rapidly come to your aid with answers to any of your queries. Your association websites also offer tools and resources. In addition to AASL's website, also check YALSA's and ALSC's, depending on the ages of your students. LM_NET has thousands of school librarians around the world who share information and respond to questions. My own School Librarian's Workshop Facebook group is a growing forum that functions much the same way.

Additionally, you have a personal learning network. This includes librarians with whom you have become friends over the years and nonlibrarian friends who have different backgrounds and interests that might prove helpful. For example, I was looking for yoga exercises for people who had limited mobility. I could have done a web search, but it was much faster to contact a friend who has been practicing yoga for years and is well acquainted with what is available in the area, as well as the subject in general. She pointed me to some possible locations but also located some excellent chair yoga exercises and a television program that could be recorded. Not only did I get a fairly rapid high-quality answer, but my friend felt good about being able to help.

Specific Leadership Skills

Almost every discussion of leadership identifies vision as something that distinguishes all leaders. You created your vision in Chapter 2, and that will be what inspires your library program; but you will also need to demonstrate vision in other ways. If you decided to create a Makerspace program in your library, you had a vision of what it could be. Because it was compelling and exciting, your administrator approved your plan.

When you show yourself as a visionary in such situations, you are using your expertise power. Your awareness of the current trends and developments in technology, your knowledge of new web-based resources and apps, and your understanding of what is happening in education on the national scene (your professional associations are a big help here) allow you to create new programs, help teachers integrate the most appropriate tech into a curricular unit, and sometimes keep administrators informed. This is visionary leadership.

The best leaders lead by example. It's not "do what I say," it's "look at this and you can do it, too." You lead by example all the time. Think of all the resources you use when you work with classes. At the upper levels, teachers are witnessing what you are doing. In elementary schools, you can send teachers a synopsis of what you did with their class and include links to anything you created, along with a note letting them know if they are interested, you will show them how to do it themselves.

How you deal with people who come into your library is leading by example. You don't demand respect from your students. You get it by giving them respect. Learning the names of the custodial staff, especially the one(s) who clean the library shows you value everyone and adds to your message of the library being a safe and inviting place for all. Honoring teacher confidences and letting your administrator know when a teacher does an outstanding project with you (and praising the teacher's work) are all ways of creating a positive environment by example—and it will be noticed.

Leaders motivate others. Students who regularly get poor grades reach a point where they are unwilling to try, believing it would be wasted effort. Bright students are so fearful of not getting a top grade they avoid taking risks and go for a safe route, never learning the value of challenging themselves. Because you work one-on-one with students as they work their way through a project, you are the one who can help them discover they are smarter than they know and can do more than they believed. Because you are the "expert" and you respect them, they trust you.

The same is true with teachers. Many are intimidated by technology. Erroneously believing their students are digital natives and therefore know everything about tech, teachers too often hesitate to use much in their teaching for fear they will not do it well and their students can do it better. Through your example and helping them along the way, you motivate them to try new things and become more self-confident about using these resources.

Because you can draw on your unique knowledge and understanding of tech trends, you can present a vision of where you want to take students (and teachers) through the library program. Your clarity and well-researched support for your latest concept can capture the attention of your administrators, becoming a motivation for them to support you as you take the library program into new territory.

Allied with motivation is empowerment. Knowledge is power, and whenever you learn something new, you feel empowered. When you motivate teachers to try new technology or work with you on essential questions, you empower them. Their self-confidence becomes a springboard for continuing to learn how to integrate more technology and techniques into their teaching.

You empower students in the same way. Showing them they can learn on their own and follow the path of their interests is the first step toward lifelong learning. When you guide a student to just the right book to read, you open the door to a love of books. We know kids who read succeed. This means more than reading the homework assignment or the required book for class. They learn to read in the classroom. You are the one who helps them discover that reading is fun, a source of pleasure and knowledge. In creating lifelong readers, you empower students for the rest of their lives.

RELATIONSHIP BUILDING

Of the five bases of power, the best one to use is referent power. This is the one where people like being around you, and because of that, whenever an opportunity arises, they will choose to work with you.

Coercive and reward power draw on a sense of fear and are highly negative. The power of expertise, which can be a big help to you, is fleeting since it usually focuses on something specific you know how to do that others want or need to learn. Referent power is an ongoing source of connection with others and it's the one you want to use most often.

How do you develop referent power? It begins with building relationships. Your tasks can wait. They will get done. Never miss an opportunity to create or expand a relationship. Always remember, first and foremost, we are in the relationship business, and if you don't know how to build relationships, you will be out business.

Consider why one librarian is successful and another isn't. They can both work in the same district. Their training and years on the job can be about the same. The successful librarian might even be a newbie with lots to learn and the other with many years of experience. Somehow the library program of one continues to grow and flourish while the other languishes. Teachers resist using it, and when they do, they prefer to handle their students without any help from the librarian. At the elementary level, the closest they come to the library is when they drop their students off and pick them up.

"People don't care how much you know until they know how much you care." I have seen this favorite quote of mine attributed to a number of different sources, but the oldest citing I have gives Theodore Roosevelt the credit. What is important is that it is true.

On the most basic level, librarians don't have the luxury of not liking someone on the staff. The job responsibility requires you to get along with everyone, which is not always a simple task when there are people who grate on your nerves and never have a nice word to say. Yet it can and must be done. But beyond getting along with everyone, it's necessary to have relationships with them. It's not always easy, but you can master the skills.

Relationships with Students

You don't grade them. They are not "yours." If they don't like you, they will not only make it obvious, they will make your life miserable. Discipline problems grow, and from your principal's perspective, you cannot manage your "classroom."

While any kid can act out on a bad day, that should not be the norm. Remember, when you give respect, you will usually get it back. Many librarians don't realize how often they disrespect a student. An adult comes in, and they break off any conversation with a student, making it obvious to the student that they consider adults more important and worthy of their time.

You help teachers find information, but you direct students where to go or give them a mini-lesson. Yes, you are there to teach them, but are you following up to see if they found what they needed? Wouldn't the lesson work just as well if you gave it and modeled the steps with them?

Do you make an effort to get to know students, particularly those who come into the library frequently? Do you know their interests—the books, authors, and activities they like? Have you ever said to one of them, "I'm so glad you came in. We just got some new books, and I have one I am sure you will like. Do you want to see it?" Students, like everyone else, appreciate when you show you know who they really are.

Relationship with Teachers

The first rule in building relationships with teachers is to respect their confidences. The grapevine and gossip is alive and well in every school. You cannot be a contributor. Relationships are based on trust, and repeating what you are told about someone is the quickest way to destroy any trust you have built up.

A core group of teachers everywhere are chronic complainers. They complain about the administration, their fellow teachers, and their students. Don't get sucked in. You can say, "I understand how you feel," or "I get how angry you are." But never agree with those sentiments. You can be sure it will be broadcast throughout the school. With PARCC testing, more teachers than ever are complaining, and you undoubtedly have the same sentiments. Saying, "I know how hard everyone has been working. It's been stressful," is perfectly fine. Notice you don't add how difficult it has been for you. That comes off as whining, and it never works.

Slowly get to know teachers' personal interests, hobbies, and whatever they care about. If you find a website or a Pinterest board you think they would like, share it with them. The more communications and connections you have with teachers, the more likely they will be open to collaborating with you.

Administrators and Board Members

This group is probably the most challenging for you to develop relationships with, and yet as power stakeholders, they are the most important. Begin with your principal. Listen to what he or she says at faculty meetings and in other communications. What seems to be of most importance to him or her? High stakes test? Integrating technology? Community outreach? How can the library program help attain it?

Figure out how to present that information in less than five minutes (they are always heavily pressed for time), and show what a team player you are and how vital the library program is. You can also find out about their personal interests, just as you did with teachers. If you see a pertinent article in a magazine, such as *Educational Leadership,* mark the pages, and put a sticky note on it, saying you thought the article would be of interest.

Unless you know them personally, the best way to get to know board members is to go to board meetings. See if you can get the other librarians in your district to take turns attending meetings. Which board member seems to be most likely to support libraries? Perhaps you can send that person, with your principal's approval, a quarterly or annual report. Be sure it is visual and shows students at work. Keep the information channel open. Issue invitations, and learn more about their interests.

Your Colleagues

How well do you know the other librarians in your district? If at all possible, you should try to have monthly meetings. Offer to host them in your library, but eventually see if you can rotate them so you get familiar with each other's libraries.

Look for opportunities to have a luncheon or dinner together. While it may not be convenient during the school year, it may be possible at the beginning or end of the year. In a social setting, you can get to know each other's interests and strengths. This extends your PLN, and if you need a quick answer or a resource, one of them might have it with just a phone call or e-mail to get you an immediate response.

Visit the public library, and introduce yourself to the children's or YA librarian, depending on the grade level you serve. Become familiar with its layout and programs. Offer to take back any promotional materials to share with students and teachers in your building.

Invite the librarian to come to your library and be introduced to your students and teachers. Be sure to let your administrator know what you have done and when your guest is expected. Learn about this librarian's interests as well. You may have areas in common to share. Ask for ways in which you can be of help. See if you can showcase student work in the public library, and then promote it on your website.

If there is a community or four-year college in your district, make a similar connection with the librarian there. Having a college librarian speak to high school students can be very impactful. They will believe him or her far more readily than they will you. Perhaps you can organize a field trip to their library so students can see what a college library looks like. It is usually quite an eye-opening experience for them.

Over time these connections will get stronger, forming solid relationships. They will enrich your program as much as you enrich their lives and programs. And remember, "People don't care how much you know, until they know how much you care." Build relationships first, and everything else will follow.

BEING LIKEABLE

Since referent power is central to your becoming a leader and having people want to work with you, it's imperative that you do everything possible to maximize that power. Creating relationships improves your referent power but you can do even more. You want people to like you.

Being liked sounds simple enough, and for some of you, it comes completely naturally. Others may in the moment make a sharp retort or use sarcasm. You can't and shouldn't change who you fundamentally are, but knowing what it is that makes people likeable, and practicing those techniques will take your far.

When you talk to people, whether it's a student, teacher, parent, or administrator, look them in the eye. You might be surprised to discover how many people, look down or away. It's equally necessary to look at those speaking to you. Check yourself to see if you are not making eye contact.

When someone speaks to you, ask some questions back. It shows you are listening. Conversation requires a minimum of two people. When in a group, don't dominate the conversation but do show you are paying attention to the ones speaking by asking clarifying questions. In seeing colleagues in the halls, a friendly, "How are you doing today?" or "What are you planning to do on vacation?" are ways of being sociable. It shows you are not too absorbed in your tasks to think of others.

Don't get distracted with other activities. When you are with another person, don't check your cellphone. If a student comes to you in the library and asks a question, don't use this as an opportunity to open junk mail or make a quick check of your e-mail. Multitasking through a conversation implies you are not interested in the other person.

Be honest. Don't fake an interest in an effort to be liked. You always need to be yourself. If you hate the idea of camping, and a teacher loves it, don't pretend you would like to go on a camping trip. You can say, "I have never wanted to go camping. What do you like so much about it?" That is showing interest without faking your own preferences.

Notice you were honest but open minded. Judgmental people are not likeable. You can't have a discussion with someone who has already made up his or her mind. You may have noticed that during election season, you don't really have a conversation with someone who fiercely holds an opinion that is dramatically different from yours. You aren't going to change your mind, and neither are they. There is no basis for discussion.

While that intensity is one reason for the adage about not getting into political discussions (especially in a school environment), it should serve as a warning about how not to be in your conversations at work. You need to be willing to listen and be open to changing your opinion.

Don't confuse being likeable with always being "on." If you are the one who is doing most of the talking, and it's often about you, you are shutting others out. You don't need to take center stage. You will be more likeable if you put others in the spotlight.

Kindness is often in short supply in this world. Look for ways to be kind to people. A handwritten note expressing appreciation means so much when we do most of our communication by e-mail or social media. Small gestures of kindness go a long way.

Related to kindness is saying "thank you," but adding a specific reason. Saying what you appreciated the other person did gives the thank you more meaning and sincerity. This also applies to compliments. It's nice to hear "You did a good job," but it's much more meaningful to be told, "Your presentation really highlighted so many significant ideas and gave me some thoughts about what I can do."

As said earlier, smiles are important. They can make someone's day. Again, this doesn't mean you go around with a sappy grin on your face all day long. But when a student comes over to you in the library or you meet a teacher in the hall, smile in greeting. And make sure that smile reaches your eyes rather than being a fake facial gesture. A rabbi once said, "The world is a mirror. Smile at it and it will smile back."

Touching students is usually not acceptable in the school environment, but you should have a sense of whether it's okay to give a quick reassuring squeeze to someone's shoulder. As humans, we crave physical contact, but justifiable concerns about inappropriate behavior has made this risky today. Of course, you can use touch with your fellow teachers, but do ask for consent. Say, "I'd love to give you a hug. You seem to need one today. Is that alright?" Usually it will be, but you never know what is in someone's past that makes them stiffen at any unexpected physical contact, and you need to respect that.

If you stand with your arms folded tightly in front of you, you are signaling you are "closed." Leaning in a bit indicates your interest. Our body language is always sending messages to others. Record yourself speaking to someone if you can. Is there an edge to your voice? Are you communicating annoyance, impatience, or judgment? All that can be conveyed in your tone of voice.

Honesty, sincere interest, and genuine liking of others will have students, teachers, and everyone else liking you. For more information on how to be likable read the online post by Travis Bradberry on Forbes.com.[3]

KEY IDEAS

» French and Raven identified Five Bases of Social Power in 1959.
» The five are: legitimate, coercive, reward, expert, and referent power.
» Legitimate power comes from holding an autoreactive title.
» Coercive and reward powers bring negative results.
» Expert power tends to last as long as others need your expertise.
» Referent or charismatic power is long lasting, and is based on people wanting to be with you.
» Leaders need to know their powers and how and when to use them.
» Take stock of the skills you have to help you focus and use your expertise power.

» Each of you bring your personal knowledge, whether it's from a field outside of education or from your hobbies and interests.
» Your tech know-how is more varied and extensive than anyone else in the school.
» Since you see students from one year to the next and keep up-to-date with what's happening in tech and education, you have a big-picture perspective.
» In addition to the print and online collection in your library, you access vast resources through your PLN and your state and national associations, which provide an array of information.
» Because of your knowledge and awareness of current trends, the latest tech resources, and the bigger picture you can present a vision of where to go that is compelling and attracts others.
» You lead constantly by example.
» Your one-to-one teaching and interactions motivate others to go beyond what they thought were their limits.
» In motivating teachers and students, you empower them to go beyond what they thought were their limits, creating lifelong readers and learners.
» In addition to building your relationships, you need to ensure you are likable.
» Look people in the eye while having a conversation with them.
» Don't multitask when talking with someone.
» Be honest, but not judgmental.
» Smile genuinely, be kind, and make your compliments specific.
» Learn when and how to touch someone.
» Check your body language and your tone of voice.

Notes

1. French, J. R. P. Jr. and Raven, B. "The Bases of Social Power." Retrieved from https://books.google .com/books?hl=en&lr=&id=lOTrBQAAQBAJ&oi=fnd&pg=PA251&dq=French,+John+R.P.+and +Bertram+Raven.+%E2%80%9CBases+of+Social+Power.%E2%80%9D&ots=wQLHj02MEZ&sig =mqmtp9TIRz3Z3H1WhC0QaAf-zTw#v=onepage&q=French%2C%20John%20R.P.%20and%20 Bertram%20Raven.%20%E2%80%9CBases%200f%20Social%20Power.%E2%80%9D&f=false.
2. Van Vliet, V. "Five Forms of Power by John French and Bertram Raven." ToolsHero, February 2, 2014. Retrieved from www.toolshero.com/leadership/five-forms-of-power-french-raven/.
3. Bradberry, T. "13 Habits of Exceptionally Likeable People." Retrieved from www3.forbes.com/ leadership/13-habits-of-exceptionally-likeable-people/?kwp_0=60676&utm_campaign=13-habits -of-exceptionally-likeable-people&utm_source=FacebookTest1&utm_medium=referral&utm _content=3&kwp_4=339437&kwp_1=215902.

CHAPTER SEVEN

IMPROVING YOUR LEADERSHIP EXPERTISE

Improving your leadership skills and expertise must become an ongoing activity. No matter how successful you are, you can always get better. If you are not growing, you are contracting. You can't rest on your laurels because life is ever changing, and you will always need new strategies to meet those changes.

In his book, *Good to Great: Why Some Companies Make the Leap . . . and Others Don't,* James C. Collins compellingly argues that good is the enemy of great.[1] His reasoning is when you are good and know it, you tend to become complacent. To be great requires constant drive and discipline.

Another business book, *If It Ain't Broke . . . Break It: and Other Unconventional Wisdom for a Changing Business World* has a similar message.[2] Assuming all is well because everything seems fine can set you up to be blindsided by change. The business world sometimes seems obsessed with trying to anticipate "What's next?" but there is an important lesson for us in education. In your personal life you can and should live in the "now," but you can't afford to do so with your library program.

The total upheaval in the school library world that occurred with the onset of the Great Recession at the end of 2007 should be a stark reminder of what happens when we get too comfortable. Librarians had lived with very small budget increases and occasional budget cuts, but no one dreamed that libraries and librarians could be eliminated. The paradigm was that schools have classrooms and a library, so therefore they have teachers and a librarian (or two).

That belief got blown away as district after district all across the country cut and eliminated librarians. Elementary librarians who thought they were untouchable because they covered teachers' contracted duty-free periods, discovered the administration was able to find another way to provide that time. In high schools, two librarians became one, clerks disappeared, and too often even the one librarian position was cut.

The bottom line is you have to prove yourself every day. You must always be open to new learning and what you can bring to your students and teachers to improve learning and student achievement. It's all about continuing to grow as a leader.

You are on your first steps in your progress to becoming an outstanding leader in your school, possibly in your state, and hopefully on the national level. Don't look on your growth as an arduous task, but rather as an exciting journey that will widen your perspective and understanding. Every day is a new adventure. Embrace it.

TO DO AND TO DON'T

Leaders know how to manage their time—they have to. Remember one of the stories you told yourself as to why you couldn't be a leader? You didn't have time. As you take on more tasks and responsibilities, you can quickly find yourself overwhelmed. Even with good time management, you can get swamped. You just need to know how to minimize those times as well as some techniques to get your life back in order.

You almost undoubtedly have days when you feel you will never get everything done. Mostly, it's a matter of finding out what organizational techniques work best for you. Then you must become sufficiently disciplined to use them.

No one has more than 24 hours in a day. Realistically, you need time to sleep, eat, and be with family and friends. That leaves a limited number of hours to get everything done. Yet if you look around, you will see that some people do it very well, and others are constantly floundering.

The truth that you know but hate to face, is that you are probably wasting a great deal of time. It's getting easier and easier to do so with lures, such as Candy Crush or other Facebook games, checking e-mail, or looking at posts on your social media of choice. Procrastination has also always been with us, but more avenues are now available.

Take an honest inventory of your habits. Make a list of how you squander time. What tasks do you avoid doing for as long as possible? This is not meant for you to blame yourself for these habits. Even the most organized people need downtime. You can't shift from one task to a dissimilar one without a brief break of some type. The brain doesn't work that way. The challenge is not to turn that brief break into an extended waste of time.

Make another list of your daily routines and others you do on a regular basis. Which ones require a deep focus and which are "no-brainers?" It is important to be cognizant that all tasks are not equal in how much concentration they need. You should know what time of day you are best suited for the ones that involve the most attention so that you can deal with them at the optimum time for you.

Think about how you spend your average workweek. I sometimes characterize many librarians as using a fire extinguisher and duct tape as their prime tools. They are spending much of their time putting out fires or patching up problems. That's draining. For the most part, it is caused by not having a mission and vision (which you now have) or setting goals for attaining desired objectives. As the great philosopher Yogi Berra is reputed to have said, "If you don't know where you are going, you will wind up someplace else."

Stay focused, and be productive by finding a way to have a to-do list that works for you. Some highly obsessive, motivated people can have one list for the day with all tasks prioritized. They consider completing it a mark of their success.

The nature of your job makes it unlikely that you can do that. Your days tend to be very unpredictable. Consider a weekly to-do list. I have one that is for two or three days. I have a column on the right where I list the different categories of my tasks. For you, it could be "back room" for tasks such as cataloging, ordering books, etc., "administration" for doing reports, and "teaching" for getting materials for a class. You would be the one to best set the categories.

I put stars next to my high priority tasks. Another way is to identify tasks by whether they take concentrated time or can be done whenever you have a few free minutes. Writing a report is one that takes focused time. If you stop in the middle, you need to review what you did before continuing. Checking e-mail can be done between complex tasks.

Some of you will find it most efficient to keep your to-do list on your phone or tablet. Others prefer a traditional pencil and paper to have it in view all the time. This is not one-size-fits-all. How you organize your available time is personal and must fit your personality, work style, and your situation. Keep experimenting until you find the one that works best for you.

EMOTIONAL INTELLIGENCE

Successful leaders have high emotional intelligence (EI). In 1990, Peter Salovey and John D. Mayer wrote an article for *Imagination, Cognition and Personality* on Emotional Intelligence. Dan Goleman, a psychologist and science writer, published a book by the same title in 1996. The business world took note.

In essence, EI is about how well you recognize, understand, and manage your emotions, and how well you perceive, understand, and influence other's emotions. You need to have both parts to have a "high" EI, and those who do are skillful leaders. If you can deal well with your emotions and that of others, you build more effective and lasting relationships, and as noted earlier, relationships are the key to developing advocates for you and your program.

In his work on EI, Goleman identified five key areas of emotional intelligence: self awareness, social awareness, self-management, relationship management, and self-motivation. The first four are interconnected, as the first two are about recognizing emotions, and the next two are about regulating emotions. While the first and third refer to one's self, the second and fourth are about the social connections. Together those four make for a complete understanding of the not-always-recognized role emotions play in our lives and our success.[3]

Self-Motivation arises from a combination of self-awareness and self-management. As you understand your emotions—those that drive you and those that stop you—and are able to manage your negative emotions, you have the tools to be self-motivated.

Self-Awareness means you recognize your own emotions in the moment. While you may know you are angry, unhappy, annoyed, or any number of emotions, unless you recognize what has triggered those feelings, you are apt to respond in ways that bring negative results. Recall the last time you became really angry. What was the cause? How did you react? Was the outcome satisfactory? What could you have done differently?

Identifying your emotional triggers and coming up with ways to manage them can help you prevent outbursts that take a long time to fix. This is not to say your feelings aren't justified or that you should bury them. You can't begin to deal with them unless you are aware of why and how you react strongly. As you become more successful at identifying your own emotional responses, you develop increased self-confidence in your ability to handle difficult situations.

Social Awareness is being able to perceive the emotions of others. It can prevent you from saying something at the wrong time because the person you are speaking to is very upset. You must become an active observer of body language, and to some extent, voice. Just as a person's stance communicates much, a tightness in how they are speaking can also alert you to their emotional state. You learned about this in Chapter 3 on classroom management. Empathy and active listening are vital to developing social awareness.

Become attuned to what someone cares deeply about. A person's job satisfaction has little to do with money (unless they are severely underpaid). It rests on their feeling fulfilled and valued. I once made a major error when trying to be helpful. I had just taken a job as head of a school library with a staff of one co-librarian, a secretary, a clerk, and a circulation desk clerk (lots more money then). My predecessor had the clerk doing a large number of tasks. In an attempt to lessen her work load, I gave the job of doing the bulletin boards to the circulation desk clerk, never realizing it was the clerk's favorite thing to do.

I was more successful in recognizing my co-librarian's attachment to the shelf list file, despite it being fully automated. I kept it up until she retired, giving her full authority over maintaining it. My biggest mistake was in moving too fast before I had fully gotten to know what motivated my staff.

Empathy is part of social awareness. When you recognize a message in someone's body language, communicate your concern. I noticed a teacher friend walking with shoulders slumped and chin pointing down. When I asked how she was doing she said she had an argument with her department chair, but I knew it was more than that. I invited her into the library for coffee and told her I was sure that was not the real cause of her unhappiness. She broke down and told me about her son becoming addicted to heroin.

Active listening is hard to develop in today's world. We are so concerned with what we want to say next, we don't pay complete attention to what the other person is saying. Repeat what you heard to verify you understood. Respond honestly, respectfully, and without judgment.

Self-Management begins when you recognize your triggers and develop techniques for managing them so you aren't ruled by your emotions. When in a confrontation situation, people tend to go to a defensive or offensive response.

Neither is effective. When you get defensive, you are quietly blaming yourself while making excuses, which puts you in a weak position. If you become offensive, you invariably escalate the conflict. The better approach is to discount the tone and any accompanying rhetoric and focus on the underlying message. Calmly react to that.

I had a teacher storm into my library not long after I took charge of it. She had learned that her barcode was her social security number (this was in the days when only numbers could be used) and she was livid. My first internal response was, "I didn't set up the system. I just got here. Why is it my fault?" Instead, I said, "If you give me a day, I can change that. I will print out a record of what you have borrowed for your class, mark them as returned, change your barcode to the last five digits of your social security number, and re-sign the books out in your new number."

She was mollified. I had taken the wind out of her sails by not arguing back. At the end of the school year, we changed all teacher barcodes. And that teacher became a strong supporter of the library, using it heavily with her students.

Other techniques for dealing with emotional triggers include doing something physical, such as taking a walk, the familiar mental exercise of counting to ten, or having a mantra you can count on to get you back in focus. Some people find journaling helps—but don't let that encourage you to wallow in self-pity. Another alternative is to talk with your mentor if you have been wise enough to get one. Just don't complain to others in your building. This is about you learning to manage your emotions, not adding to the school gossip.

Relationship Management describes how you work with others. With volunteers and any staff you might be fortunate enough to have, you want to be a team builder. The relationship piece implies you have the skills to first build the relationship before you attempt to manage it. You get to know the members of the team—what they want, what is important to them, and what makes them feel successful.

Whether you are chairing a committee or are a member, be alert for situations that raise conflicts. You can lead from the middle by knowing how to diffuse confrontations before they escalate. Active listening helps. If you remain calm and restate what you believe you heard from each of the parties, you can identify the specifics of the differing views. You can then help the group focus on the goals of the committee. More often than not, this will reduce tensions and let everyone breathe easier.

Recognize that despite our belief in the importance of dealing with issues logically, 80 percent of our decisions are based on emotions. We tend to use logic for the 20 percent that justifies our conclusions. It can clearly be seen in political situations where people cite many logical reasons for their choices, but in all honesty, it was first an emotional reaction.

Advertisers and marketing companies are well aware of the role our emotions play in purchasing decisions. You can look at ads for cars, food, and even insurance to see how they are designed to play on our emotions. Even when the text is a logical sales pitch, the images are directed straight to an emotional response.

The emotional root of decisions is probably at the heart of why the countless research studies on the positive effect of school librarians and library programs on student learning are ignored. Administrators, boards of education, and politicians have emotional memories of libraries. These are not always pleasant and are based on images of a library long gone from the scene. When they make decisions to cut the budget or the entire program, they are operating from an emotional conviction that libraries are the stodgy book warehouses of the past.

The only way to get past those entrenched emotional responses is to write a new story to replace it. Successful librarians are now creating reports that are highly visual, which automatically sends an emotional message. Making sure students are a part of the reports, preferably talking about what they are learning and doing, increases the impact of the message.

Snapshot Days, sponsored by a number of state library associations, capture the versatility and broad use of libraries around the state. School libraries are invariably invited to participate, as ALA has recognized the importance of all types of libraries working together to send a single message of how libraries transform, and public libraries are responding as well. (See the ALA website www.ilovelibraries.org/librariestransform.)

You cannot be a successful leader unless you can manage your own emotions. You need to manage your frustrations and annoyance when your contributions are overlooked. People will follow you when they realize you care about them but don't have to be on guard against any emotional upheavals from you. When you are able to manage your emotions and recognize feelings in others, you can skillfully handle relationships—whether one-on-one or in group situations.

Although not a component of emotional intelligence as described by Salovey and Mayer, nor in Goleman's work on it, safety plays an important role in whether people will trust you and in establishing relationships with them. Simon Sinek gave a TED Talk entitled, "Why Good Leaders Make You Feel Safe," directed primarily to business people.[4] He spoke about a Congressional Medal of Honor winner who was asked why he risked his life to save others. Like many in the military, he responded that they would do the same for him.

Sinek sees this response as originating in caveman days when our world held dangers from predatory animals and assorted other sources. In essence, we drew a circle of safety around those who lived with us, and the multiple threats to our existence lay outside this circle. Within this circle were people we could trust to have our backs, and we would have theirs.

Advance forward to modern days. While corporate America has many negatives, at one time people felt secure in working for a large company, knowing they would have a job for life. This changed toward the end of the last century, accelerating when the economy hit a tailspin in 2008. Layoffs abounded. It became a dog-eat-dog world, and you couldn't trust your coworker not to stab you in the back to protect his or her job at the cost of yours.

Some companies didn't follow that harsh structure and benefited heavily from employee loyalty. Education today has taken on some of the negative characteristics. Faculty feel threatened from outside and from within the education environment. Morale has suffered tremendously.

View the TED Talk and be able to show a new aspect of leadership by making your library a safe haven for your fellow teachers. Do what you can to have their backs. Keep what they say confidential. Be ready to provide resources that might help them in difficult situations.

Leadership has many components. EI is one of them. The more you raise your EI, the greater your referent power. And as you know, referent power is the strongest in getting people to want to work with you.

As you grow into your role as a leader, you will continue to discover more ways to show your leadership. Some are already natural to you. Others you will hone over time. It's a journey.

LEADING AND MANAGING

Just as the meaning of mission and vision are often blurred and used interchangeably, so too are leadership and management. In the business world there is usually a clear-cut distinction between the CEO who is the leader and the COO (Chief of Operations) who is the manager, but that is a matter of titles. The five bases of power is a reminder that because someone has authority, it doesn't make him or her a leader.

Even in the business world there are far too many "leaders" who, in some critical ways, function as managers. The underlying reason is that leaders take risks and by definition risk carries the possibility of failure. There is such a fear of failure that people will go through hoops to avoid it and instead prefer to manage than put themselves out in front and lead.

With the heavy emphasis on testing, along with the stresses students have about getting into college, they are being taught to fear failure. But there is never achievement without some failure. James Bryant Conant (1893–1978) is reputed to have had a sign on his wall saying, "Behold the turtle. He makes progress only when he sticks his neck out." The quote is attributed to him, but I have never been able to verify it.

Four-star General Colin Powell, former Secretary of State and member of the Joint Chiefs of Staff, has wonderful quotes about leadership. In his Lessons in Leadership (www.au.af.mil/au/afri/aspj/apjinternational/apj-s/2011/2011 -4/2011_4_02_powell_s_eng.pdf), number 15 is particularly relevant:

> *Part I:* "Use the formula P=40 to 70, in which P stands for the probability of success and the numbers indicate the percentage of information acquired."
> *Part II*: "Once the information is in the 40 to 70 range, go with your gut."

Powell's advice is don't take action if you have only enough information to give you less than a 40 percent chance of being right, but don't wait until you have enough facts to be 100 percent sure, because by then it is almost always too late. His instinct is right: Today, excessive delays in the name of information-gathering lead to analysis paralysis. Procrastination in the name of reducing risk actually increases risk.[5]

If you search online, you will find numerous definitions and images for the distinction between management and leadership. There will be many similarities, but there are differences as well. For me, a simple one is that management is about consensus building and being a team player. Leadership is about making decisions, and this frequently involves taking risks.

One of the best comparisons I have found shows the two as parts of a jigsaw puzzle. It looks at how leadership and management complement each other in their roles, focus, approach, methodology, style/tone, and outcome.[6] The leader's role is innovative, setting the vision (which you have done earlier). The manager carries out the mission (which you also wrote). A leader challenges the status quo, while the manager works with the status quo. A leader takes the long- term view. A manager works in the here and now.

You can also view the leader as one who works strategically. Everything (or almost everything) is directed toward achieving a long-range objective. Managing is what you are doing from day-to-day. For some of you, this is not part of an overall plan. You are swamped and work hard to carry out all your tasks. When these tasks aren't connected to a large overall plan, they are unfocused and don't necessarily bring you closer to accomplishing your mission or achieving your vision.

When you create a strategic plan, which will be discussed in Chapter 9, you develop an action plan that enables you to achieve your goals. The action plan provides the tactics you employ daily—or on the time line you created—to meet the goals that were set.

So when the question arises, should you lead or manage? The answer is, in your world you need to do both. The combination of leading and managing contributes to blurring the distinction between them. To be effective, you need to be aware of when you are leading and when you are managing. You also have to be honest and know when it's time to step away from managing and be a full-fledged leader. And that happens when you need to take a risk.

You also are leading when the risk proves successful. At that time, you give those who work with you the credit to make it happen. If the risk fails, you are the one who takes responsibility. That's leadership. Sounds scary, and it's why so many "leaders" don't really do the job. But if you take a number of risks and most prove successful, you build credibility. The idea is to build your bank of successes by starting with the no-risk or low-risk projects previously discussed.

A quote, usually attributed to Winston Churchill notes, "Success is walking from failure to failure with no loss of enthusiasm." No one has an unbroken streak of success. If you don't try something new—and occasionally risky—you miss the chance to learn and the chance to succeed. If you want your library program to thrive, you have to move it out of the status quo. Doing that entails risk—and leadership.

MAKING MEETINGS MATTER

Most people hate meetings. In schools, teachers dislike faculty meetings. They come at the end of a long day, they last too long, and most of the time, it seems they are held because that's the day for the faculty meeting. There's nothing worse than having to attend a meeting because that's when you always have it, unless you are leading that meeting. I am sure there are times when the principal has to scramble to find items for the agenda.

Many school or district committee meetings are equally boring, and too many of them are on a regular schedule whether there is business to accomplish or not. There are always a few people who monopolize most of the time, while others sit and doodle. At the end of the meeting you don't know what got done other than getting the next meeting scheduled. And then you are back again at a meeting being held because it's on the calendar.

Managing relationships when you are a member of a committee is diffi-cult enough, although you now have some ideas about what to do. As you become more of a presence in your school, you may be asked to chair a com-mittee. This article has some excellent pointers on how to build your skills as a facilitator: http://smartbrief.com/original/2016/08/shine-leader-strong -facilitation-skills. When you run your own meetings, how the other partici-pants view it is up to you.

Before the first meeting is scheduled, be sure you know what the committee is expected to produce and by when. What resources will you have to achieve the goals? Who else is on your committee? You might know some individuals and have positive or negative feelings about them.

For those who you think might cause a problem, plan potential solutions in advance. What strengths do they have that you might be able to utilize? Giving someone a job or responsibility encourages cooperation. Reach out ahead of time to those you don't know. Introduce yourself, providing a bit of professional and personal information and invite them to do the same.

Develop an agenda, send it out before the meeting, and invite feedback. The sooner you can get people participating, the more quickly and efficiently the meeting will run. If the comments that come back to you seem to be off focus, put them at the end as "additional recommendations." This gives you most of the meeting to set the course and still acknowledge those who took time to respond. If the others feel those suggestions are not relevant, put them in a "parking lot" in case they might connect to later work by the committee.

If at all possible, provide snacks and drinks, and get folders and pens for the committee members. Put a label identifying the committee on the outside of the folder. Inside the folder, include the pen, the agenda for the first meeting, and a list of the committee members. The cost to do this is negligible and people feel good about getting these little gifts. It also creates a "let's get down to business" feeling that will get the committee moving forward from the start.

Begin the meeting on time even if some people haven't arrived as it's respectful to those who have shown up on time. If too many people are late, you can suggest that the start time for the next meeting be adjusted so that everyone can make it without unnecessary rushing. Even more important is to end the meeting on time. This practice respects that the members have lives and makes them feel more positive about the committee.

Include the goal of the committee at the top of the agenda and the goal/purpose of the current meeting. The first item of business for the first meeting is introductions, but keep them brief. To do so, give them a time frame such as, "We have one minute each to introduce ourselves." If someone goes on too long, you need to rein him or her in very politely. Say something like, "Thank you for sharing so much about yourself. I am hoping we will get to know more in subsequent meetings." That will effectively end the long ramble.

Have a large easel pad available. It helps if you can get a committee member to serve as the scribe throughout the meeting. While most people will have a tablet to take notes, this keeps what is happening visible, and you can use it to send out minutes of the meeting to the members. You might also need to report on what was accomplished to administrators, and this way everyone gets the same information.

After the introductions, review the goal of the committee and when the task is expected to be accomplished. At future meetings, begin the same way, including what progress has been made to that date. Having a regular opening to the meeting settles everyone into work mode. Next, identify the purpose of the current meeting—which, along with the overall goal, is at the top of the agenda.

As you work your way through the agenda, you should be the one to get the discussion started, but don't dominate the conversation. This part is about managing. You want everyone to feel heard. Keep track of who is and isn't speaking. Draw the quiet ones in by asking their opinion. Ask someone who talks a lot to scribe the big ideas raised. This gives them something to do besides talking.

If at all possible, have interim tasks for committee members to perform before the next meeting. Depending on what is to be done, a member may be working alone or in a small group. Set up a Google Doc for them to report on what they have accomplished. This way, they are held accountable, and you can monitor how much is getting done. If someone hasn't posted anything, contact them and find out if they need help. This way you are seen as supportive, rather than critical.

Set the date and time for the next meeting before you adjourn—on time. Use the notes on the easel pad to write up the minutes of the meeting. Post them on your Google Doc and ask for any comments, changes, etc. Give a due date by when suggestions must be submitted. After that, send the finalized minutes to any administrator expecting a report, and post it on the Google Doc as well.

For the next meeting and all the ones to follow, send the proposed agenda out in advance or put it on the Google Doc. As usual, ask for the committee members' input. Again provide snacks and drinks. The first item now on the agenda is a review of what was accomplished since the last meeting.

When the committee completes its overall goal, celebrate with pizza or something similar. Thank everyone for working so diligently to reach this point. Find something positive to say about each committee member. Give a few members the task of putting together a final report of what was achieved. The cover sheet should include all the members and possibly the special contributions of each. Purchase attractive folders and give each committee member a hard copy of the final report that you also send to the administration.

Reflect on what you personally have accomplished. You used both leadership and management skills. You created a collaborative work environment, and you demonstrated to your administration that you are a leader.

KEY IDEAS

» Leadership is an ongoing learning experience.
» Most people waste time, which leads to feeling overwhelmed.
» You cannot shift from one type of task to a very different one without taking a break. Your brain requires it.
» Don't extend the needed break by getting caught up in nonproductive uses of your time.
» Identify the jobs that require focused time and those that can be squeezed in whenever you have a few free minutes.
» Find a way to keep track of the tasks you need to get done that fits your personality, work style, and situation.
» Emotional Intelligence (EI) is about how well you recognize, understand, and manage your emotions and perceive, understand, and influence others' emotions.
» The five areas of EI are: self awareness, social awareness, self-management, relationship management, and self-motivation.
» Self-Awareness, social awareness, self-management, and relationship management are interconnected with each other as the first two are about recognizing emotions and the next two are about regulating emotions. Or connecting differently, two are about one's self and the other two are about social connections.
» Self-Awareness means you recognize your emotions and what can trigger negative ones.
» Social Awareness is about your ability to identify the emotions of others.
» Self-Management is the ability to keep your emotions from causing you to react negatively in the moment.
» Relationship Management entails understanding how to successfully interact with one person or a group to affect a positive outcome.
» Our decisions are based primarily on our emotions. To elicit a different decision from one person or key stakeholders, you need to alter their emotional response to it.
» People are loyal when they feel safe. A good leader knows how to create a circle of safety that makes people feel secure.
» The distinction between leadership and management is blurred by many.

» There are those with the title that goes with being a leader who refuse to take the risks that are a part of leadership.
» Leaders who delay making a decision until they get all information from every side (focus groups and such) suffer from "analysis paralysis."
» Managers are consensus builders and team players; leaders are innovators and decision makers.
» Leaders take the long view and set strategic goals; managers focus on the day-to-day, accomplishing the tasks that will achieve the strategic goals.
» In the library setting, you need to be both leader and manager, but you need to know when you should be leading and when you should be managing.
» Build your success bank by making many no-risk or low-risk changes, giving you the credibility necessary for eventually taking larger risks.
» When you chair a committee, be clear on what the overall goal is.
» Reach out in advance of the first meeting to the committee members you don't know, and prepare a strategy for managing the ones you know might prove difficult.
» Send out your proposed agenda in advance of the meeting, inviting feedback.
» Include the goal of the committee and the specific goal of the meeting on each agenda.
» Start and end each meeting on time.
» Have someone write the big ideas on an easel pad to keep them visible throughout the meeting and to use for writing up minutes of the meeting.
» Have tasks for members to do in preparation for the next meeting, and ask them to report on them on a Google Doc.
» Begin all meetings the same way to settle everyone down.
» Review what was accomplished since the last meeting.
» When the committee completes its task, compile a summary of what was achieved into a final print report.
» Give a copy to each member and to the administration.
» Being a committee chair requires you to both lead and manage.

Notes

1. Collins, James C. *Good to Great: Why Some Companies Make the Leap . . . and Others Don't*. (NY: HarperBusiness, HarperCollins, 2001), 1.
2. Kreigel, Robert J. and Louis Patler. *If It Ain't Broke . . . Break It: and Other Unconventional Wisdom for a Changing Business World*. (NY: Warner Books, 1991).
3. "Daniel Goleman's Five Components of Emotional Intelligence." https://www.sonoma.edu/users/s/swijtink/teaching/philosophy_101/paper1/goleman.htm.
4. Sinek, Simon. "Why Good Leaders Make You Feel Safe." TED2014, Filmed March 2014. https://www.ted.com/talks/simon_sinek_why_good_leaders_make_you_feel_safe?language=en.
5. Hararim, Oren. *Quotations from Chairman Powell: A Leadership Primer*. GovLeaders.Org. http://govleaders.org/powell.htm.
6. Champions for Growth: Leadership Coaching. *Leadership AND Management*. January 7, 2013. www.championsforgrowth.com/leadership-and-management-complimentary-partners-forever-connected.

CHAPTER EIGHT

KNOWING HOW TO HANDLE IMPORTANT COMMUNICATIONS

Your leadership skills are growing. You are stepping out of your comfort zone and taking on additional responsibilities. There are more balls in the area to juggle. More people are observing you. Some are judging, others are admiring.

While you will never be able to manage all of it every single day, your ability to prioritize and focus on what is important will help you be successful. You don't want leadership to become overwhelming and cause you to step back. Don't look for perfection. You won't achieve it. Just look for ways to improve and do things better next time.

COMMUNICATING IN PERSON

The ability to communicate clearly is an important leadership quality. It's part of emotional intelligence. It comes into play when you are leading a meeting, and of course it is intrinsic to building relationships. However, with so many communication channels now available, the art of being a good communicator has become increasingly complicated and carries potential pitfalls.

Face to Face

Despite all the electronic means of communication, you are always meeting people in person. Some are planned, others happenstance, and many are random—barely registering on your consciousness. Yet all of them tell people something about who you are.

You might have a scheduled meeting with an administrator at their request or at yours. If it's the administrator who has set up the meeting, you will probably be told the reason for it. Review any information related to it in advance. Bring copies of all relevant facts and documents with you, along with a tablet or whatever you prefer for taking notes as you may be asked to do some follow-up.

Show up for the meeting five to ten minutes early. Let the secretary know you have arrived. When you are shown into the office, warmly greet the administrator and get settled as quickly and efficiently as you can. If others are part of the meeting, try to position yourself so you can see everyone.

If it's natural for you, offer a smile, but don't fake one. Let the administrator start the meeting. Recall your active listening skills. Listen attentively without thinking of how you will respond. When it's your turn, if appropriate, recap what you understood the administrator to have said. Take a moment to think through any answer before you rush in to speak.

When you have a question, be succinct. It's not necessary to give a lot of details unless you are asked to do so. At the conclusion, review with the administrator anything you were directed to do and find out the deadline to complete the tasks.

For meetings you schedule through a secretary, specify the purpose of the meeting and how much time you would like to have with the administrator. As before, show up early and fully prepared. Briefly restate the purpose or the meeting. If the administrator wants more details and/or background he or she will ask for it. If you are bringing a problem, be sure you are also bringing a possible solution. End the meeting within the time limit you set.

Sometimes, when planning a collaborative unit, you and the teacher decide to have a face-to-face meeting. Preparation, active listening, and being open and friendly contribute greatly to a successful outcome. If you know in advance what the teacher wants to do, assemble any relevant resources and share them when needed. Take notes, offer your suggestions, and always defer to the teacher's preference. At times, the teacher's concept is too fact based, requiring little in the way of critical thinking or serious research. Don't criticize the idea, but instead show the teacher how the project could be "expanded."

If the teacher hasn't told you his or her plans, be prepared to help create the project on the fly. Ask about the essential question and the final project. You might need to work together to come up with both of these. Point out any websites and apps that might support the project. In both situations, follow up with an e-mail summarizing what the two of you planned.

For casual meetings, such as a teacher dropping by or meeting someone in the hall, don't act too rushed to speak with them. Even if you are busy, there is always time to greet people warmly. In the first situation, find out if the teacher wants something and let him or her know when you will get to it if you cannot do so immediately. When you see them in the halls, you both are probably on your way to somewhere else, so a quick greeting suffices, but make sure you at least acknowledge them with a smile and a brief comment. If they seem to want more, ask them to drop by the library so you can give them the attention they deserve.

Random meetings are those when people you may not know show up in your library or elsewhere. If they come into your library, of course you will ask if you can help them. Even if they don't want any assistance, keep an eye on them to see if they are finding what they need. The reason for mentioning this type of in-person meeting is that every occasion is an opportunity to present yourself as a leader and your program in the best possible light.

On the Telephone

While the phone is not truly a face-to-face communication tool, it does have the same immediacy, and you can hear tone of voice, which is always important. You may think the telephone is archaic in this day. Certainly our students don't seem to use it at all, but you still receive phone calls and they are more likely to occur in the professional setting. Unlike the telemarketers who besiege you at home, the ones you get in school tend to be important.

Because you turn to the telephone so rarely, you may need to pay some attention as to how you present yourself when speaking on the phone. When you receive a call, identify yourself by your full name and title. It is the professional way to respond.

The caller will identify who they are, although you may recognize the voice. The tendency is for you to multitask, checking e-mail or looking for something on your desk. Just as with your other interactions, use your active listening skills. If it's hard for you to focus, take notes. When the other person is finished, you will be able to respond specifically.

Be clear as to what you are to do based on the call. Do you need to get back to that person? By when? Put it on your calendar.

Identify yourself as well when you are the call initiator. Be very succinct in what you have to say. If more information is needed, you will be told. When you have to leave a voice message, keep it brief again. Add you will call back and say when you anticipate that will be.

On a call, obviously people can't see you. They will be making subconscious decisions about you based solely on your voice. While you want to be brief, you don't want to be brusque. Smile when you are speaking. It will show up in the tone of your voice.

WRITTEN COMMUNICATION

The most frequently used form of communication in school is e-mail, however, you may also find a need to text. The least common form of written communication today is snail mail, but it has a time and place. Knowing when to use it can add to your reputation.

Via E-mail

You administrators use it. Your colleagues in other schools send you e-mail message. Vendors do as well. Your in-box fills up quickly on most days.

When answering e-mails, consider the recipient. If you are replying to an administrator or a parent, be extremely mindful not only of the content, but also grammar and spelling. The safest course of action is to write it first as a Word document so you can easily check it for errors before pasting it into the message box.

Reread your message before you hit send. Without any verbal clues, you want to be sure what you said cannot be misunderstood. Although you might use emoji's in your casual e-mails, they are inappropriate for these messages, so your words alone must make your intentions obvious. The same is true when you initiate an e-mail to these recipients.

Never use e-mail to criticize someone. It will come back to haunt you. If you have an issue with the IT department, communicate it verbally to your administrator. As many politicians and business people have learned, e-mails are forever. I was once called by the HR department of a school system and asked about a librarian who had worked with me and listed me as a reference. Because there was confidential information involved, and I wasn't going to give the person an excellent rating, I e-mailed back a request to be called. It's much safer and far more professional.

Copying and blind copying other people can also cause problems. If you text a complaint to the IT department, don't copy or blind copy your administrator. It will be seen as tattling.

Avoid sharing jokes, and definitely don't forward political messages to your teacher and librarian friends in the district. You may know them well and share political views, but it's inappropriate in the school setting. Use your personal e-mail for that.

Forwarding messages also needs special care. It is wise to delete all identification about the person who sent it to you, the others who they sent it to, and any of the original senders of the message. This ensures that you keep their information confidential.

Sending a Text Message

You rarely send text messages within the school setting unless it is common in your building. One reason is the only smart phone you are likely to have is your personal one. However, there are some occasions when you will use your own phone in the professional setting.

Most commonly, texting occurs when you are meeting with someone who is either going with you to another location or someone is coming to visit your library. It is normal in those cases to exchange cell phone numbers to ensure you can contact each other in the case of an emergency.

If you and your administrator are going to a meeting outside your building, it may be necessary to give each other your cell phone numbers. Text him or her to say when you have arrived, are leaving, or have been delayed. While text shorthand may be very natural to you, don't use it in these messages. After the event, don't use the administrator's phone number for any further school or personal business. It would be inappropriate.

It is a good idea to avoid "text talk" if you are communicating with an author or other guest coming to your school. If you would like to hang on to that person's phone number, as a courtesy, ask permission. We need to be more careful about guarding each other's privacy.

By Snail Mail

Leaders know the importance of making a lasting impression. Handwritten notes mean more today than they ever did. In an era where speed is expected, snail mail takes time. Choosing a note card, putting pen to paper, thinking of the right words, and sending it off requires much more thought than dashing off an e-mail or leaving a text message.

You know it will take a few days for the recipient to read your note, so there's that interim time when you wonder how they will react. Usually, it's with surprise and appreciation. When someone receives a note in snail mail, it is noticed. They recognize the time you put into it.

I have been recommending that librarians send a follow-up thank-you note after an interview, mentioning something of importance that was said, preferably by the recipient. Written thank-you notes have become a thing of the past, but that has only strengthened their impact when you send one. Before our current technology changed our communications so drastically, receiving a thank-you note was expected and hardly noted. Today, the recipient is flattered you took the time.

Something wonderful happens in someone's life and they post it on Facebook. Within minutes their friends from around the country post congratulatory messages that are quickly "liked." But if it's someone special in your life, send a snail mail note of congratulations. They will treasure it long after the Facebook posts have been forgotten.

Get well and sympathy messages are the same. The recipient may get fifty or more comments on Facebook, but the one they will remember will be the handwritten message sent by snail mail. If it's a colleague in your school and they aren't taking time off, you can put the note in their box, but using the post office is even better.

When you use snail mail, you realize how little thought you give to all the messages you send off in the course of a day. Speed is of the essence and you rarely ponder your words. If you use your smart phone, half the words come up for you to click on since you use them so frequently. Relationship building is not a race. It takes time and attention. Using snail mail is one way to deepen your connections with others.

DIGITAL COMMUNICATION

Having good communication skills used to mean verbal and written. Today you need to be able to send your message in multiple ways, and each requires different skills and often a different mindset. Contrast a written note with e-mail. They both are written, but what you say, how you say it, and the strengths and weaknesses of each are very different.

When you look at digital communications, the dissimilarities among them abound. Each is viewed in its own way by the reader. You need to be aware of what each does well and recognize which is the best vehicle for your message.

On the Web

What is the "face" you present to the public? Whether it's the school library web page, Twitter site, or your blog, this is how students, teachers, administrators, parents, and anyone who looks up your library online sees who you are. What you post and how it looks tells the public a lot about you.

If you maintain a web page, how often do you update it? Formats can look dated fairly quickly. As with anything else, if you see the page often, you don't realize how it has lost its original shine. What looked good when you first put it up, now seems very "yesterday."

How easy is it for users to find what they are looking for? Consider whether the overall look is inviting. Just as "in" colors change with every fashion season—making what you had before look old—so too do the color scheme, fonts, and graphics for web design.

Make it a habit to look at web pages of school libraries. Which ones capture your attention? Why? What message are they sending about the library and the school librarian? How are they doing that? See what you can use or adapt for your own web page.

See what these librarians promote on their site. There should be a good mix of easy-to-access information for students, including databases and links (possibly using Symbaloo), LibGuides, or other resources for current assignments and ongoing needs, and library news. Many librarians also have Pinterest boards on assorted topics, including new books or suggested titles to read. As part of outreach, good school library web pages also have information for parents.

Many of you are constrained from updating easily by your tech department. Usually it's because they are expected to do most of the work. Talk with them. Show them the great web pages you have found. Share what you would like to be able to do, and open a dialogue as to the best way to achieve it without burdening them.

If you maintain a Twitter page for your library, what does the banner look like? It needs to be a blend of books and tech—and students. Take some time to craft your profile. You want it, along with the banner, to convey the message of what a twenty-first-century library looks like. Be sure you know and follow the procedure for posting student pictures online—whether on Twitter or your web page.

Consider how often you want to tweet. Writing 140 characters is not an onerous task, so you might want to do it every day or so. But text alone will not have people following you. You should also have some visual content, and that takes time. You want to tweet on a fairly regular schedule so that you hold interest. With some trial and error, you can determine what works best for you.

Keep an eye on your tweet activity shown on the right of your Home page. You can see how many impressions you received and can identify the top tweets. This is excellent input as to what people are interested in. The more "retweets" you get, the better.

Blogging is another way to send out your public face and your message about your library program. It can be part of your website or completely separate. If it is separate, have a link to it on your home page.

As with your web page, your blog's page must have a current look. Fonts have gotten cleaner, and you want to include pictures and graphics (being very careful to observe copyright). Think of what you want to call your blog. There are many excellent library bloggers out there. Among my favorites are Buffy Hamilton's *Unquiet Librarian,* https://theunquietlibrarian.wordpress.com; Doug Johnson's *Blue Skunk blog,* http://doug-johnson.squarespace.com; Jennifer LaGarde's *Adventures of Library Girl,* www.librarygirl.net; and Joyce Valenza's *Never Ending Search* in *School Library Journal,* http://blogs.slj.com/neverendingsearch. (And my own blog which comes off my website, https://hildakweisburg.com/blog.)

When you read these and other library blogs, you realize the bloggers focus most on an aspect of school librarianship. Buffy Hamilton apprises you of collaborative projects she is doing with her teachers and how this furthers students' critical thinking. Not all her posts are about this, but it forms the majority of them. My blog, as you might guess, focuses on leadership.

What do you want the focus of your blog to be? Would a blog name help to promote it? Once you have that set, think how often you want to write a blog. It can become an overwhelming task. I do mine once a week, but once a month is reasonable for you to undertake.

Blogs are very public. While you will never be perfect, do proofread. Spelling errors and other grammatical mistakes can creep in, especially when you feel under pressure to get the blog done and posted. It's better for it to go up a day late with no errors than having your mistakes be online for all to see. The good thing is, you can make corrections if you spot them later.

Sending a Report

Some of you are required to send regular and/or annual reports to your supervisor. Even if you don't have to do them, make every effort to use this communication vehicle to promote your program and the impact it has on student learning and teacher growth. So many librarians complain their principal doesn't know what they do. How are they supposed to find out if you don't tell them?

You should send at least an annual report and try for quarterly ones as well. Before you begin to put it together, consider what you want to feature. Data is great, but the number of books circulated is very old school and is particularly worthless at the elementary level where students are expected to check out two books at every visit.

What data showcases your program? Look to see what students have produced in the library. If you have a Makerspace, you definitely want to report on that. You may have a book club or have organized a Battle of the Books. These are features of the library program you can highlight outside of people's perception of what you do all day.

At the middle- and high-school levels, keep track of the different departments who used the library for student research projects. You may not have art or music classes visit as frequently as English and social studies, but their occasional presence—which will show up again on your year-end report—demonstrates how the library program contributes across the curriculum.

Start a list of unusual research questions students ask and what the answers were. It will show the breadth of your program, as well as the deeper thinking that students are being guided to undertake in the library. Also obtain the statistics on how many times your databases were accessed. (If you don't know how to do that, your vendors will help you.)

Preparation for your report should be ongoing. Take photos and make videos of students and classes at work. Record student comments about what they are learning and how they feel about working in the library.

When you are ready to write your report, look for the format that will best carry your message. Obviously, the one format you don't want is a heavy text-based report. That style is dated and looks like you haven't moved out of the last century. Even if you put all the numbers up front, the odds are that your supervisor will only skim it.

Choose a web resource for digital storytelling. Issuu.com has been around for a while. It allows for text, but you can also include photos, graphs, charts, and infographics to make the data come alive. Piktochart.com is another excellent tool for creating a highly visual report.

A relatively new entry is Microsoft's Office Sway at Sway.com. It was one of the twenty-five sites selected for AASL's 2016 Best Websites for Teaching and Learning. This is what the committee said about it:

> Office Sway is a great tool for creating interactive reports, newsletters, presentations, and personal stories. All the user needs to do is upload content and then select a design. Sway does the rest! Easily add video, music, pictures and more to enrich the interactive component and take advantage of Sway's suggested search result features (pulls in tweets, images, and other relevant content). Formatting is automatically taken care of and templates can be swapped with ease. Creations are easily shared online and privacy settings help you determine the breadth of your audience. A good website for use with grades 5–12.

Check the AASL page on Best Websites for Teaching and Learning (www.ala .org/aasl/standards/best/websites) for other digital storytelling resources, and choose the ones you like best for making your reports. Not only will they be read when you use a visual format, you will also be demonstrating your expertise as a technology integrator.

MAKING A PRESENTATION

At some point in your leadership journey, you will need to make a presentation. While the thought of speaking before a group is the last thing some of you want to do, it need not be a fear-inducing experience. You have information and expertise you need to share. While one-on-one is fine in your daily life, there are times when you must address a larger audience.

For your first foray into public speaking, see if you can address a known group, such as a department or grade-level meeting. Ask to make a short presentation—between 15 and 30 minutes. Choose a topic you are familiar with and can explain easily; it may be one or two websites or apps you have been using. It will be of help to teachers as well it you want to introduce a new database so teachers will incorporate it into their assignments.

Prepare a slide presentation using Prezi, Power Point or some other tool with which you are comfortable. Your slides should not be text heavy. Think of the slides as cue cards, reminding you of what you want to say. Screenshots are very helpful as well.

As you plan your presentation for teachers, focus on why you think it's important to bring this information to the attention of your audience. What will they gain by knowing about it? In what way will it make their life easier?

Next, outline the steps for using the resource. Present each one on a separate slide. This will allow your audience to follow along without getting sidetracked or confused. Identify anything that might seem difficult for a first-time user, and take special care reviewing how to deal with that piece.

On your title slide, have a screenshot of the home page of a web resource or the opening screen of a database, depending on your presentation. Adapt this idea for whatever else you might present to an audience. The next to the last slide should have participants discuss their big "take-aways" and what they would still like to know. When speaking to a group of your colleagues, the last slide should be a reminder that you are always available to help if they have any questions when they begin using the resources on their own. For other groups, provide your contact information.

Whether you are giving your presentation in your library or at some other location, always check out the technology well in advance of your start time. Things do go wrong, and you need to be ready to move to Plan B. Be sure you have sent your slides in whatever format you are using in advance to those who will be attending your presentation, and ensure everyone has access to computers, tablets, etc., so they can follow along and take notes.

Begin your talk as closely as possible to the announced start time. Give everyone a few minutes to access the presentation. You may be switching from your slides to the resource. If you need to do that, explain to the attendees how they can do the same.

Thank the group for inviting you and bring up your presentation. Even though most of your audience will be focused on their own computers or tablets, do look up regularly to scan the group. It will clue you in as to how engaged they are and whether some of them are having difficulties. Since you *never* should read your slides word for word, you really should have a separate speech that no one sees. It makes your presentation more interesting. I write mine on a printout of the slides along with my predicted time for each slide. After a while, you become quite comfortable with ad-libbing along with each slide.

After you have given a few such presentations to teachers, you are ready to try talking to people you don't know as well. The parent association is a good next step. Each time you do a presentation, you become increasingly comfortable with the format and confident in your own abilities.

RECOGNIZING THE MESSAGES YOU SEND

The more visible you become, the more people will be noticing what you do. As librarians, we try to create a warm, welcoming safe environment for our libraries. We also want our students to become lifelong readers and learners. But often there is a disconnect between these desires and what our students perceive. Most of us are so busy, we are sometimes on autopilot, doing things without thinking, not realizing our actions are sending a very different message than we intend.

Years ago, I was hired to consult for a district hoping to improve its library program. (Unfortunately, we don't see that anymore.) I walked into one elementary library with the intention of seeing how its arrangement helped or hindered creating an inviting atmosphere. I didn't have to look far. On several walls, there were large posters proclaiming library rules. No loud voices—speak in whispers. Wash your hands before reading a book. Sit properly in your chair. Raise your hand before speaking. Only two books may be checked out.

I wanted to leave. The library was neat and orderly and completely cold. It was about rules, not about reading, not about discovering exciting new things. I am sure the librarian never intended students to feel what I was feeling. She probably also had her hands full many days with students who found the environment so repressive they acted out. I hope she didn't punish them by not letting them take out a book.

At a high school I visited, I was also struck by how a beautifully designed facility could be a turn off. The rules weren't posted in the same way, but there was no indication that this was a place for kids. The few posters were formal purchased ones. The walls had no added color. There was no student art, and no bulletin board showcased student accomplishments. The message was, "This is a place run by adults and you are not to disrupt it." Not surprisingly, there were almost no students working individually, and I discovered teachers rarely brought their classes in.

Numerous elementary librarians, intending to instill a sense of responsibility in students, have a strict overdue policy. If students don't return their books on time, they can't take out any more. The message kids get is "returning books on time is more important that having something new to read." While overdue books are a problem since the books can go astray and parents are expected to pay for lost books, there are other ways to handle the situation. You can have slips ready to insert into a book pocket or even taped to the cover informing parents to please search for books not returned. If it's the school that has set the rule, make sure students are directed to some books to read while their classmates are selecting theirs and checking them out. Send home a note about the missing titles, and allow the student to borrow books as soon as the overdue ones are returned, even if it's not the class's day in the library. Make it about getting books to read in the hands of students.

Creating lifelong readers is being hampered in many places by the emphasis on Lexile scores. It's fine for instructional purposes but not for recreational reading. The idea is to make reading fun, not challenging, hard work. Leisure reading levels are usually *below* instructional levels. This builds fluency and enjoyment, which then allows students to take on more difficult texts in class. I dislike the "five finger" rule. If I had to look up five words on every page of a book, I wouldn't want to read it. I prefer a "no-finger" rule. This would mean there might be a few words in the book that would be new, but for the most part, the students could zip along and enjoy the story.

Some students want to read a book that's well above their Lexile level. Frequently it's on a subject they are interested in, such as a sport, or it could be a popular title. Even now, you might get a third grader who wants to read a *Harry Potter* story and is really not up to the task. The tendency is to not let the child borrow the book. I would let it go out, suggest sharing the reading with a parent or older sibling, and recommend another easier book also be borrowed. The stretch in trying to read the harder text will only improve the student's reading skills. This is different from forcing a child to read a harder book to match a Lexile level. This is a personal choice.

There are many ways unintentional messages are sent. When you stop speaking with a student to take care of a teacher or an administrator who has entered the library, you are telling the student that adults have a higher priority. Students note that they are not allowed to eat in the library, but at social gatherings held in the library, adults eat and drink—and spill.

Consider the restrictions and rules you have. What messages are they sending? What purpose do they serve? Many schools are now permitting food in the library as long as students clean up after themselves, and allow drinks in covered containers, although these are usually forbidden near computers.

THE IT DEPARTMENT AND YOU

No one in the school system uses more technology than you do. The computer tech teachers come close, but they rarely use as broad a range as you do. From your automated system to your databases, to the various resources and apps you incorporate into your teaching, you are constantly accessing different technologies. You may have a website you maintain for the library. If your district permits it, you might have a Twitter account and use Pinterest and/or Instagram. Technology is intrinsic to almost everything you do.

And then there is the tech department that manages—and controls—access to all the tech in the district. It's often a love-hate relationship between the two of you. Depending on how you are handling it, sometimes it's all hate. Unfortunately for you, you can't afford to let that happen. The tech department is too powerful, and if you can't turn the relationship around, the tech people will be a constant roadblock.

From the Tech Department's Perspective

To change your mindset, look at the issue from the tech department's point of view: There are a limited number of them on staff, and the faculty and administration are always needing them to attend to an issue *immediately*. When everything is functioning properly, no one ever praises them. As soon as something goes wrong, blame is heaped on them.

The tech department is charged with safeguarding the integrity of the system, but students are forever trying to get around any firewalls they construct. Teachers (and rarely students) don't always think before opening e-mails, and inadvertently download malware and viruses. The bandwidth is limited and too many people want to stream videos. The tech department is in a no-win situation.

Then you come along. The school year starts and you need them to get any newly purchased database uploaded to all your computers. You want students in the incoming class entered into your automated system. New teachers need to be entered as well. If your ILS system has had an upgrade, you want the tech department handling that immediately as well.

Research projects during the year may have you making quick calls to the tech department to open a site the filter has blocked. You may need them in order to make modifications to your website. They try to keep everything organized and handled in order by requiring you to fill out a ticket, but you want them to realize you have immediate needs and can't wait for them to get around to dealing with it. By the time they open the blocked site, the kids are through with the project.

Going from Conflict to Partners

How can you turn this around? You need to start building a relationship with the tech department, and the best time to do it is when things slow down. If at all possible, set up a meeting with them during the summer to discuss how you can help each other. And bring food to the meeting.

Make a list of the jobs you need the tech department to do and put them in approximate chronological order. Ask if you can be trained in doing some of them yourself so as not to strain the department's limited resources. In my last library situation, we loaded all the new students and teachers into our system.

Let the department know that whenever a research project comes up, you will explore potential sites ahead of time to identify which ones might be blocked so they have advanced warning and time to unblock the sites. That said, see if they can find a way to "fast track" any requests from you to open sites if some are discovered while the assignment is under way. Explain why it is so important while showing you recognize their concerns and problems.

Find out if the head of the tech department is a member of ISTE. If you are as well, you can use that as a common bond for discussion. You might even attend the ISTE conference together. When you come across articles or resources you think would be of interest to the tech people, preferably online, send it to them.

If you haven't done so already, see if you can get on the district's Tech Committee. You need to show your tech competence and that you recognize and value the service given by the tech department. When you become part of their solution instead of their major problem, you will have found a valuable ally in ensuring your program runs smoothly and meets the needs of students and teachers.

KEY IDEAS

- » Show up 5 to 10 minutes ahead of a scheduled meeting time with an administrator.
- » Let the secretary know you have arrived.
- » Bring all relevant material with you, along with a device or pad for recording information and any follow-up you are to do.
- » Listen to what the administrator is saying without thinking about how you will respond.
- » Pause before answering to gather your thoughts, but be succinct.
- » At the conclusion of a meeting, review the highlights and what you are supposed to do as a result of the meeting, along with when it is due.
- » If you bring a problem to the meeting, also have your proposed solution.
- » For casual meetings, such as a teacher you meet in the hall or someone dropping by, don't appear too rushed to speak.
- » Recognize that any in-person meeting, whether scheduled or random is an opportunity to present yourself as a leader and your program positively.
- » Give your name and title when answering the telephone.
- » Take notes to ensure you are paying full attention to the caller.
- » When making a call, after identifying yourself, concisely explain the reason for the call.
- » If you must leave a voice message, keep it brief and let the person know when you will call back.
- » Smile when you speak on the phone. It will be heard in the tone of your voice.
- » When sending an e-mail, particularly if it's to an administrator or parent, write it in Word first so you check spelling and grammar before sending.
- » Always reread e-mails before hitting send.
- » Never criticize someone in e-mail. It will come back to haunt you. If you must say something negative, do so in person.
- » Think twice before copying or blind copying someone. It often is seen as tattling.
- » Don't send jokes on school e-mail. It's inappropriate.
- » Before forwarding e-mails, delete all information regarding who sent the original and who else forwarded it. It's a matter of confidentiality.

» You may use text messaging in the school setting if you are going to another location with an administrator or colleague, or someone is coming to visit your school.

» Ask if it's all right to keep a colleague's or visitor's phone number after an event. It's a matter of respecting their privacy.

» Snail mail is such a rarity these days that the message has a greater impact than ever before.

» By writing a thank-you note, a message of congratulations, or a condolence note, you take much more thinking time than if you dashed off an e-mail message or a Facebook post.

» Your website, Twitter account, and blog are among the ways you present yourself digitally as the face of the library program.

» Refresh the look of the library web page so it doesn't become dated. If necessary, work with your tech department to determine the best way to do it.

» Your banner and profile on Twitter say a lot about you and your program. Take time to be sure it sends the message you want.

» Tweet on a regular basis, but don't overdo it. You want to have something valuable to say and show when you do.

» If you blog, keep the look up-to-date. Checking the sites of skilled bloggers will give you ideas on color, fonts, visuals, etc.

» Blog at least once a month so people know to check it regularly.

» Whether it's required or not, send reports at least quarterly and annually to your supervisor to ensure they know what you do and what your program looks like.

» Select data and information that highlights how your program benefits students and teachers.

» Use digital storytelling resources to create your report and make it highly visual.

» Speak at a departmental or grade-level meeting for your first presentation to minimize your nerves at addressing an adult audience.

» Choose a topic of interest to your audience, but one with which you are very comfortable explaining.

» Create a slide show using whatever resource for it you prefer.

» Focus first on why the subject is of interest to this audience. Why do they need to know about it? How will it benefit them?

» Have a separate slide for each step in using whatever you are showing them.

» Make a title slide using a screenshot of the resource you are explaining—or whatever would be the equivalent.

» On the next-to-last slide, ask what they will "take-away" from the presentation.

» Remind them you are always available for help on the last slide.

» The messages you hope to send and the messages students receive are not always the same.

» Rules that limit book borrowing because of overdue books suggest responsibility is more important than reading.

» Forcing kids to only read at their Lexile levels takes the joy out of reading.

» Students notice when the "no eating in the library rule" is not applied to adult social functions held in the library.

» As the heaviest user of technology in the district, you are frequently at odds with the tech department and their often too slow response time.

» You need the tech department more than they need you, so you must find a way to get into relationship with them.

» Provide the tech department with a chronological list of tasks you need them to do.

» See if the tech department is willing to give you some administrative access so you can perform a number of these tasks and take the burden off them.

PART III

PLAYING LARGER

Slowly but surely you have been becoming more and more of a leader in your building. You have made improvements to your program that have made teachers, administrators, and others begin to think of you when the district introduces something new. They know you will be able to help and make it work.

You are someone teachers can talk to and share their concerns and ideas with for trying out an idea they have heard about. You are recognized as an excellent teacher. Kids and staff love coming to the library. It's a place where exciting things happen. Not there yet? You soon will be.

Leadership is now comfortable to you. But don't get complacent. Even leaders can get too used to their new status quo. Remember, "Good is the enemy of great." You may have a larger comfort zone, but it's still a comfort zone. It is time to stretch out even more. Take your leadership to the next level.

What's next for you and your program? In Chapter 9 you find out how to create a three-year strategic plan to further not only your mission but your vision, as well. Your emotional intelligence and improved skills at building relationships have given you a core of advocates. Learn to expand on that.

Craft a tagline to get the word out about your program to a wider audience. Discover how to build your brand—and just what that means. Then alone, or preferably with some strong library supporters, put your strategic plan into action. You just might win an AASL Award with it.

Chapter 10 is about taking the steps to ensure you are seen as vital and indispensable to power stakeholders and others. You want to be valued as a core component of the educational program. Everyone, from students through administrators, parents and others, recognize how your library transforms learning and the entire educational community. Your program makes everything they do better.

Staying current now means more than just trying out the latest tech resources. It means you are aware of trends that will impact the library and education—whether they come from technology or the business world. In order to make this happen, you will have to read in new areas.

We come to the end in Chapter 11. It's called "Maintaining Joy" because it's important that in taking on all your new roles and responsibilities, you don't burn out and find yourself overburdened by tasks. To be a successful leader, you must keep your passion alive and greet each new day with enthusiasm. (Honestly, this doesn't mean every single day. Some are more of a challenge.)

How are you going to do that? First and foremost, you will accept that you don't have to do it all. Others can help. A good leader knows how to delegate. Your well-being depends on it.

You also can now begin to give back. You benefited from the experience of others as you grew as a leader. It's your turn to help others. Write proposals to present not only at your state conference, but at national ones as well.

It's time to run for office in your state association. Participate more fully on the national level. Oddly enough, by giving back, you will accelerate your own learning, because a leader never stops learning.

Finally, you need to give yourself the "gift of time." If you are always giving, you will eventually drain the well. Work is not the most important part of your life. Don't neglect what matters most.

CHAPTER NINE

ALWAYS HAVE A PLAN

↗ **Planning is fundamental to success. Flying by the seat of your pants might work** in a pinch, but it's not how you move your program ahead. Always have projects that you would like to put forward when the time is ripe. You never know when an administrator has extra funding, is looking for a creative way to spend funds, or you discover a grant opportunity.

I once had a superintendent who laughingly said to me that she always felt as though once I had one project under way, I had several more ready to go. She was right. Administrators have people to whom they must answer, and sometimes they need to put an idea into action within a very short time. It will serve you well for your administrators to know you always have something on the back burner that you can quickly organize.

Your planning process will go much smoother if you have some basic groundwork in place. You already have your mission and vision, which are basic to all planning. There are some other building blocks as well. Once you have developed your brand and have become adept at writing a tagline and knowing when and where you need one, you will see that it's easy to focus on goals and the specific of creating a solid plan, including a two- to three-year strategic plan.

YOUR BRAND AND TAGLINES

Brands and taglines are essential to the business world. From corporate America to small start-ups, companies worry about their brand. Depending on who they are, they seek to be household names or equally well known within their sphere of activity.

Taglines are so ubiquitous you absorb them without noticing. That is their particular power. Used together taglines with brands can be powerful vehicles for making stakeholders aware of your program and its value.

Brands

Businesses have always known the importance of their brand. They zealously guard it from infringement by others. More recently, public librarians have come to appreciate the value in having a brand and have been developing them, but thus far, few school librarians have made the attempt.

In part, this may be due to not understanding what a brand is and why it is a vital component to have the library program recognized as indispensable to the school community. To understand branding, it's best to see how the business world defines it. According to the online *Business Dictionary*, it is:

> The process involved in creating a unique name and image for a product in the consumers' mind, mainly through advertising campaigns with a consistent theme. Branding aims to establish a significant and differentiated presence in the market that attracts and retains loyal customers.[1]

What does this mean in library terms? You have a unique name. It's the name of your library. You may or may not have a logo—but it's great if you do. Once you create your brand, you might see if some students in an art or entrepreneur class can design one for you. Check library websites for examples..

A consistent theme occurs when you use a special font or other identifiers that alert people that the message is coming from the library. Think of how many Oreo cookie variations there are. What do they all have in common? Why didn't Nabisco just market them under new names? The answer has to do with the value of a brand that sends a message to the consumer about what they will receive if they buy the product.

Nabisco's reasoning ties into what a brand means. It's a promise to the consumer. It's something they can count on. They have already developed positive feelings (and remember the importance of emotions) about the product, so they are open to considering variations. It does help if the brand at least subliminally carries an emotional message.

Going back to the definition of a brand, it is also a way you identify how you are distinct from your competitors. One of the biggest challenges school librarians face is convincing stakeholders that the school library program is unique. You want them to know it provides learning opportunities that no one else in the building can duplicate. If the program is eliminated, a void that can't be filled will result.

To determine your brand, the *Small Business Encyclopedia* recommends you answer the following questions:

> » What is your company's mission?
> » What are the benefits and features of your products and services?
> » What do your customers and prospects already think of your company?
> » What qualities do you want them to associate with your company?[2]

This is fairly easy to translate into the library setting. You have your mission and you can easily answer the other questions. So what is your brand? Here is an example.

> The Library—Safe and Secure—Literacy and Tech—Helping you find the right, relevant answers—ALWAYS.

What does this brand say? It has an emotional content in "Safe and Secure." Most of you have in your vison about the library being a safe, warm, welcoming environment. This must be part of your brand. Note that it's not your vision and it's not your mission. You can't get all of your roles into the brand, but you can highlight the combination of literacy and technology, which only you do. This branding also points to why the Internet and Google are not a replacement for you and your program.

You can use this brand if you wish, modify it to better represent you and your situation, or write one that fits you best. The important thing is that it resonates with you and your stakeholders. As noted, it must distinguish you from any competitors. In education, this would be the literacy coach and the computer/tech teachers. Once you have it, put it on your website without defining what it is, along with your mission and vision statements.

Check out some famous brand names and see how they promote their brand. Look for the emotional content. McDonald's often refers to itself as "The Happy Place." On their website, they are pushing that they have eliminated artificial preservatives and colors, proclaiming, "We are committed to quality," adding, "Because Your Family Matters." This is more emotional content. Why is McDonald doing this? Who is their competition? How are they differentiating themselves?

Attune yourself to messages from the business world to see how they get their message out. Use what you learn to adapt how you send out messages about the value of your library program.

Taglines

You see taglines every day and, unless you are aware of what they are, you probably don't realize it. Once you do, you will see them everywhere. Taglines are very brief, high impact statements making you think of the company (or in our case, the library) in a specific way. Unless tied to a marketing campaign, they are a form of PR to keep your existence in the minds of your "customers" or stakeholders.

In the past, they were called slogans and some still use the phrase. Here are some of my favorites:

» The best part of wakin' up. . .
» Think outside the bun
» America runs on . . .

» I'm lovin' it
» You're in good hands
» M'm! M'm! Good!
» Don't leave home without it

I am sure you can identify every one of these companies. A few of them have been used forever, including Campbell's Soup, Folger's coffee, Allstate, and American Express. McDonald's changes its tagline every so often. The best taglines hit an emotional button. Allstate's certainly does. McDonald reaches for emotion, as does Folger's. Think about the message and the *feeling* each of these brings to mind.

Companies change taglines to meet a strategic shift. When they perceive a change in the marketplace or want to hit a different emotion or sentiment, they are apt to come up with a new tagline to address it. Lowe's used to have "Let's Build Something Together." Now it's "Never Stop Improving." My theory is they want to go beyond what can be construed as building and emphasize all the ways you can improve you home. In other words, they are looking to attract a wider market than those who consider themselves DIY enthusiasts. Give some thought as to which you prefer and why.

It's not enough for people to see the name of your library. They need some association to go with it. Consider what you have learned about the importance of emotion. What will make teachers, administrators, students, and parents connect to your library program?

When I still was producing my School Librarian's Workshop newsletter, I needed a tagline for it—of course. I first used, "Your Whole Library Program in Every Issue." I showed it to my daughter, who was also my business manager and knows a lot about marketing. She said it was good, but could be much better.

She asked and answered these questions: What do librarians want? They want to be valued. What do they fear? They fear being eliminated. From this, she said my tagline should be "Indispensable—Just Like You." Although this tagline was close to my brand: "Hilda Shows You How to Be Seen As Indispensable," I went with it. For librarians, my name was totally associated with my product and, therefore, a part of my brand.

Where do you put your tagline? Just about anywhere. It should go on your website, your e-mail signature, and on anything you put out under the auspices of the library—pencils with the library's name for prizes, bookmarks, etc.

Taglines tend to reflect your brand. You can pull from one aspect of your brand and promote it in a tagline. When you are reaching out to a different audience, you may want to change your tagline. Begin by creating a basic tagline, such as one of these:

» Where the classroom meets the real world
» Where reading becomes a way of life
» We go beyond our walls

You can see how each of these connects to the brand mentioned earlier. Think of other possibilities and get started on creating yours.

KNOW YOUR GOALS

The next step in planning is to know your goals. You can have a number of them. Remember, you should always have a plan, and while one given plan will focus on no more than one or two long-term goals, you should have some ready to go. At this point, you can write any number of goals. You simply need to know what you want before you start to focus.

Perhaps you want to transform your library into a learning commons. You might have smaller aspirations, such as creating collaborative inquiry-based projects with classroom teachers. If you noticed your male students are reading much less than female students, your idea could be to turn more of them into lifelong readers. The possibilities are as varied as librarians and the schools in which they work.

Why are these goals important to you and your students? Achieving them will take a great deal of work and concentrated effort. You already have a full schedule, and you will be taking this on. If the potential of realizing these goals doesn't excite your passion, all the planning in the world will not bring it to fruition. You will feel overwhelmed and bored with it, avoiding completion of the various steps. Your goals should be a driving force for you, not a drag on your time.

With your list of goals in hand, it's time to determine what you want to tackle. In particular, if this is your first venture, you don't want to overextend yourself. You always need to consider how realistic it is for you to achieve your goal. For example, if you are in a school with an unsupportive administration, antiquated technology, and no or a minimal budget, attempting to create a learning commons is most likely to set yourself up for failure.

In the same situation, you could work on raising the interest of boys in reading or in developing collaborative (or cooperative) projects with teachers. Don't discard your learning commons idea—just shelve it for a much later date. Once you have met the more achievable goals, you will have moved your program forward. The administration will have noticed what you are doing, and you will have begun changing their attitude toward the library and how you can bring positive changes to the school.

As you contemplate your goals, make another reality check. What are you risking going after them? In Chapter 5 you took on no- and low-risk projects to begin building your reputation. Now you are considering more ambitious ones. Leadership does involve risk taking, but you need to know what is at stake for you and your program.

On the flip side of the risks are the rewards. Consider the benefits that will ensue when you are successful. This is somewhat like the business practice of analyzing return on investment (ROI). You will be investing your time and your reputation. What will you get back, assuming all goes as planned? If the return (reward) outweighs the investment (risk), then this is a goal to use in your planning.

IDENTIFYING YOUR TARGETS

The targets for your strategic plan are those impacted, or involved directly or indirectly by your plan. You will have some targets that are obvious and some that are not. You need to address all targets to ensure your message gets out.

One reason the transformation to a learning commons is such a big, bold plan is that it reaches across all stakeholders, all of whom are your targets. Your primary target is, as usual, the students, as they will be using the program, along with teachers. But equally important are administrators and members of the board of education; a learning commons becomes so central to a school that it completely alters the perceptions of what a library is. And in some ways, the community at large is another target. Each of these targets will be heavily impacted by the strategic plan.

To better understand this concept, consider a smaller-scale plan of increasing collaboration or cooperation with classroom teacher units. Your first target in this case is the teachers, since you must work with them if the plan is to succeed. The second target is the students, since they will be researching in a different way from the past, dealing with both you and their teacher.

But if you are being proactive as a leader, you should consider your supervisor or principal as another target. Although the core purpose of the plan's goal is to improve student learning, an important subsidiary benefit is for the administration to recognize the vital role school librarians play in student achievement. Therefore, in some way, you must make the principal aware of the plan.

To build advocacy from parents, you want to show them the value the school library program brings to their children. Part of your plan should also include informing them of what students learned and why it was important for them to do so. In practice, your targets are the same as with the learning commons, but because the actions involved are on a much smaller scale with less publicity every step of the way, it is far more realistic to undertake this as a first step into a leadership challenge with more risk.

SOAR RATHER THAN SWOT

If you have been involved with developing your state association's strategic plan, you must have done an "environmental scan." This attunes you to what is going on around you to ensure your plan is realistic and serves your purpose. One type of scan is called a SWOT analysis. It stands for Strengths, Weaknesses, Opportunities, and Threats. The first two categories are an internal assessment and the last two are an external assessment. Two are negative and two are positive.

After doing many of these strategic plans, I recognized that the list of weaknesses and threats always skewed heavily to the negative. As librarians and educators, we do an excellent job at seeing what is not going well. While no one makes anything up, the perspective we take is always to see the adverse situations and not recognize how well we have been doing.

Working on an ALA strategic plan (or, more specifically, the plan for one large element of ALA's plan) I was delighted to be introduced to SOAR, which replaced SWOT. It changes our mindset. The acronym stands for:

» *S*trengths
» *O*pportunities
» *A*spirations
» *R*esults

To analyze your *Strengths*, consider:

» What are you doing well?
» What makes you unique? (You needed to think about that when writing your mission statement.)
» What key resources and expertise give you an advantage? (Consider the last two bases of power)

In listing your *Opportunities*, think about:

» What changes do you foresee in the future? (You can, for the moment, think of negative ones.)
» How can you create "chopportunties?" (This is where you take the negatives and see where you can use them to become a positive. It's the combination of "challenge" and opportunity.)
» What do your stakeholders want/need? (If you aren't addressing that, you won't win them over.)
» How can you highlight your strengths?

For your *Aspirations*, reflect on:

» What do you care deeply about?
» What difference do you want to make?
» What does your preferred future look like? (Recall your vision statement)
» What project/program might showcase this?

Identify the following aspects of *Results:*

» What two to three goals do I want to accomplish? (Based on what you have come up with for the first parts of the SOAR analysis, you might want to tweak your goals.)

» How will you know you are succeeding? (How are you going to measure success?)
» What resources will you need?

THE STRATEGIC PLAN

With your overall direction set, you can now get down to the nitty-gritty details of determining how you will accomplish the plan—otherwise known as working out the *tactical* details. It may help you to recognize the difference between strategy and tactics. Think back to the discussion in Chapter 7 of the difference between leading and managing.

Leaders see the big picture and hold a vision for where they want to go, knowing it will take time to get there. That's strategic planning and why a strategic plan is almost always a multiyear plan. Your goals are your strategic targets. What are you seeking to accomplish over time?

Tactics are about managing. You need to have steps that will take you closer to achieving your goal one day at a time. Unless you have a strategic goal, your daily practices will probably not get you where you want to go. And if you don't have an action plan for achieving those goals, that's all they will be—unattained goals.

For each goal you identified in the *Results* of your *SOAR* analysis, create a one-year action plan. Briefly describe what you want to do for the year to get you closer to that goal. Develop your time line for the project. Identify the start and, if necessary, the end date of each step of the project. This serves to keep you accountable for completing each step. It also keeps you on track, alerting you to any adjustments that might be needed.

Identify all who will be involved. The more internal and external stakeholders you can involve, the better. By participating, they become advocates for your program. In this example, the principal, at least one teacher, and possibly library volunteers are part of the plan. If you decide to have an end-of-year celebration for participants, you can involve more people.

If your goal is about increased reading by male students, and you decide to run a lunchtime book club as your action plan for the year, you would need your administrator's approval, so his or her name should be included in the plan. Finally, identify how you will assess the plan.

You can easily work with your strategic plan if you put it on an Excel spreadsheet. This how it would look in table format in Word:

You would then use the assessments to create your action plan for the next year. Will you be continuing the book club? Perhaps add something else, such as student book reviewers, or bringing in a male author. You can have several action plans for a single goal, but don't stretch yourself too thin. Repeat the process for your second goal (and third one if you have it).

STRATEGIC PLAN

20??—20??

Vision

Mission

Goal #1: To increase leisure reading by boys

ACTION PLAN: **Have a Lunchtime Book Club for Grades. . . .**

STEPS	WHO	WHEN	ASSESSMENT
1. Briefly explain all components of club and show principal	Me	September	It's completed and a meeting time with the principal has been set
2. Meeting with principal	Me/ Principal	End of Sept. early Oct.	Meeting goes well and club is approved.
3. Create flyer announcing club and send out	Me (and possibly art teacher)	Second week in October	Flyer complete and distributed to teachers. (Could be posted on website or sent home.)
4. Students sign up	Me and volunteers or staff (if any)	End of October	A minimum of 10 kids are signed up. If more sign up, schedule for different days of the week.
5. Book Club meets	Me and students	November through May	Meet with kids. Get their feedback and recommendations.
6. Final meeting	Me and students	Two weeks before end of school	Get kids' reaction to club and where they want it to go. Use circulation statistics to see if club members increased their reading as a further assessment.

SHOWCASE YOUR ADVOCACY PLAN

Once you have successfully executed a strategic plan, you can move on to planning on a larger scale. You want to move the library onto the center stage, making as many internal and external stakeholders as possible part of the plan. You also want to get the story to the local media. At that point, the administration will be happy to participate because they want the favorable press. You might even get local officials to be part of the culmination of whatever you plan.

You can have many short-term action plans, each of which advances one part of your goal. They may run for two to three months, so you could have three or four small projects within a single school year. Each plan would have different stakeholders involved. This would spread the understanding of your program and the support of a large range of people within and outside the school.

Most plans of this nature require funding. You can look for a grant to cover costs. The local education foundation is usually an easy grant to write. A more ambitious undertaking involves applying for the AASL Ruth Toor Grant for Strong Public Libraries, www.ala.org/aasl/awards/toor.

As the website explains:

> The grant provides funding support on a competitive basis to public school libraries—located in the United States and led by a certified school librarian—for the creation and implementation of a local public awareness/marketing campaign that promotes and positions their school library as a necessary resource in the community, tying in the theme "Strong School Libraries."

Check the website for criteria and eligibility. There is a link to the press release of the most recent winner. You can read it to see what that librarian created—it might give you some ideas to use for your project.

Winning a national award gives an incredible boost to your library program. The AASL staff routinely sends a letter announcing your award to administrators, the local press, and elected officials. In addition, some awards such as the Ruth Toor Grant for Strong Public Libraries include funding for you and an administrator (or volunteer) to attend the national conference where the award is officially presented.

While you are reviewing the website, look at the other awards AASL offers. You might find something else for which to apply. The publicity you get for winning will last a long time.

KEY IDEAS

» You need to identify your brand and create taglines to aid your planning and promote your program.
» Your brand distinguishes your program from what anyone else does in the school.
» A brand lets your customers know for what you can be counted on and should carry emotional weight.
» Put your brand on your website, but don't label it.
» Taglines are slogans that keep your program in everyone's mind so they don't forget you.
» Have a generic tagline and then create others when trying to reach a specific group of stakeholders.
» Put your tagline on everything the library publishes in print or online, such as bookmarks, reading lists, etc.
» List the long-term goals you want to achieve.
» Recognize which goals are realistic and why you think they are important to you and your program.

» Analyze the risks and rewards of going for those goals.
» Identify the targets of your strategic plan, including those involved directly or indirectly.
» No matter the size of the plan, your targets almost always will be students, teachers, the administration, and parents.
» Strategic planning usually begins with an environmental scan.
» SWOT is the traditional route, standing for Strengths, Weaknesses, Opportunities, and Threats.
» Because librarians tend to focus more heavily on weaknesses and threats rather than strengths and opportunities, SOAR is a better way to do a scan.
» SOAR stands for Strengths, Opportunities, Aspirations, and Results, seeking how any threats or weaknesses can become new opportunities.
» Decide on one or two goals you would like to achieve in the next 2 to 3 years.
» Create action plans for your goals with all steps needed to achieve it. Include everyone who will be involved, a time line showing start (and end) dates, and an assessment.
» Use the assessment of the first year when creating the action plan for the second year.
» Once you are comfortable with creating a strategic plan, try one with a larger outreach.
» Consider submitting your plan for an award, such as the Ruth Toor Grant for Strong Public Libraries.
» Winning a national award will increase the awareness of your program and the value it brings to students and the school district.

Notes

1. Business Dictionary.com. "Branding." www.businessdictionary.com/definition/branding.html #ixzz4H9WNK4Lr.
2. Entrepreneur Staff. "Branding." *Small Business Encyclopedia.* https://www.entrepreneur.com/encyclopedia/branding.

CHAPTER TEN

STAYING VISIBLE
AND VITAL

Once you are recognized as a leader, there is no going back. But you also can't stay where you are. You need to keep growing. As shared earlier, "Good is the enemy of great." Unless you are continuously seeking ways to improve your program and your skills, you will slowly stagnate and fall behind.

We live in a fast moving and changing world. Lewis Carroll was ahead of his time when he had the Red Queen say to Alice, "It takes all the running you can do, to keep in the same place. If you want to get somewhere else, you must run at least twice as fast as that."[1] It does seem we never stop running any more, but as a librarian and leader, you need to run twice as fast. On the positive side, the more you step into leadership, the larger your PLN grows so you have a wide range of contacts and resources to keep you speeding along in the fast lane.

Your colleagues—both teachers and librarians—are looking to you as a role model and a resource. The administration has come to recognize your value and count on you to help lead teachers forward as education moves further into the twenty-first century. While they may not express it, they also are grateful for your help in advancing their agenda and using your special expertise in keeping them current.

EMPOWERING STAKEHOLDERS

The AASL guidelines for school library programs has the title *Empowering Students*. "Empower" has become one of the buzzwords used in business and education. As with many overused terms, frequency blurs meaning. It is a very strong word and should be thoroughly understood so you know what you are expected to do.

Merriam Webster defines empower as "to give power to (someone)" or "to give official authority or legal power to (someone)."[2] Obviously, we use the first meaning most often, but even so, what power are we giving students? Through our inquiry-based lessons, they develop the power to learn on their own and follow their passions, knowing that they have become skilled users and producers of information.

But there is a more subtle meaning of empower. When we empower someone, we make them more confident, in control of their life, and able to believe in and trust their abilities. That is a huge responsibility. Yet if you follow your students over their years in your building, you see that is exactly what you do.

The AASL Guidelines were published in 2009, and the use of "empowering" in the title was new in the world of education. Although the guidelines didn't discuss why the word was chosen, it was on target. We need to embrace the concept of empowerment. It's an important part of being a leader.

As a leader, you need to take on this challenge. Recognize how and when to empower your stakeholders. When you bring relevant aspects of your expertise to them, they become more confident in what they are doing, and whether or not they acknowledge what you have done, they are aware that they have grown as a result.

Students and Teachers

Students, of course, are your first stakeholders, and you know how you empower them. You do so with every inquiry-based lesson, every time you expand their range of leisure reading, or guide them in their searches for their assignments or personal interest. Tune into how you are building their confidence and trust in their ability to learn on their own.

Your teachers are the next group you need to empower. To do so, analyze where they are unsure of themselves and need some help. Because of rapid changes in technology, teachers are usually not nearly as capable as you are at integrating tech resources. They are unaware of the vast range and the new resources that keep sprouting up. One librarian I know sends teachers information on one tech resource each week, offering to help them see how it can be used in their curriculum units. Knowing that you are there to hold their hand as they learn how to use new technology makes the prospect less intimidating and builds their confidence.

Some teachers are not well versed in crafting units with essential questions (EQs) and enduring understandings (EUs). As you work with them—having built a relationship so they trust you—suggest possibilities to use in a learning experience. The more you work together, the greater the teacher's confidence grows in writing the EQs and EUs on his or her own.

Finally, the importance of inquiry-based learning is being touted as important in student learning. Too often the implication is that it can be accomplished solely in the classroom. Considering that it has students select the direction of what they want to learn about a topic and invariably requires research, it can't really be limited to the classroom. But you can point out how you structure an inquiry-based unit. Working with you is safe as you do not evaluate teachers, and thus, they are willing to ask questions and learn as they go.

The strong relationships and growing history of collaboration or cooperation you have built with teachers are the foundations on which you empower them. In an era when many eyes are on classroom teachers, judging and evaluating what they do, you give them the confidence and the vocabulary to show they are valuable. And you are therefore valuable to them.

Administrators and Parents

Your next step is empowering administrators. While many work hard to keep up with changes in technology and what is happening in their buildings, too often they are even more overworked than you and the teachers. When you inform them of projects teachers have done with you— always spotlighting the teacher, as well as the students learning and their reactions—you give them a deeper understanding of how collaboration (or cooperation) is impacting both faculty and students. With this knowledge, the administrator gets to know more details of what is happening in the building than could be obtained from the few classroom observations. The added benefit is that it promotes your program.

Parents are another group of stakeholders you can empower. They are aware of the dangers their children might get into in cyberspace but lack the knowledge of how to prepare (and caution) their children for the threats of playing carelessly when on the Internet. If you give a presentation to parents on keeping kids safe in cyberspace or post helpful information for parents on your website, you empower them. Even keeping them informed about projects that classes are doing is a form of empowerment as it makes them feel closer to their children's day.

Teams

You will be leading any number of different teams. If you are fortunate enough to have a staff or volunteers, they are part of your team. The other librarians in your district are another team, even if you are not the leader of it. So are members of any committee you are on or chair. You can and should empower them.

For those working in the library with you, it's important for them to be recognized for their special abilities—whether it's how they set up a display, help search for websites, or keep the shelves organized. Show these individuals that you value their contributions by how you give them a task. Once you are sure they understand what they have to do, step back. You don't want to micromanage. You don't have the time, and it makes people feel mistrusted.

Everyone works differently, so let your helpers figure out the best way to accomplish their tasks. Ask them to notify you when they complete the task or have to leave it unfinished for any reason. Let them know to come to you if they run into a problem. Keep an eye out to be sure they are not struggling, as it may take some a while before they are willing to admit they are having difficulties.

A hands-off management style empowers individuals, but as a leader, you must balance inspiring with inspecting them. On the one hand, you want your staff or volunteers to see you believe they are capable, which gives them confidence. On the other hand, you want them to avoid making a serious error, which they will find embarrassing. If they realize you are there to support rather than criticize, they will respond well and will check in with you quickly if they have problems in the future.

Keeping in contact with the other librarians in your district empowers all of you. Whether or not you have monthly meetings (and they are good to do), keep lines of communication open. Share what you are doing, including what worked and what didn't, and invite the others to do the same.

It's likely you all benefit from hearing what lessons your colleagues at the same grade level are doing. What is less likely is knowing what happens at future grade levels. If you know what your students will be expected to do when they leave your building, you can better prepare them. Equally helpful is being aware of what students have done–and not done—before they entered your school. By better understanding where students are in their learning, and what they already know, you are all empowered to improve your program and will be seen as understanding how to prepare students for the future.

Being on a committee, and particularly if you chair it, is an additional opportunity to empower others. Chapter 7 discussed how to make meetings matter. Even though you take care of committee members in the several ways discussed, you can look for ways to empower them. For example, it was suggested you give people interim tasks. Have them write up what they accomplished. For example, in addition to commending them, make every effort to give authorship credit for these sections in the table of contents of a long report or in an executive summary or introduction.

When you empower others, you accomplish a number of positive results. Those who become more confident as a result will want to continue to work with you, becoming advocates. You are also building their leadership skills and serving as a role model. With your fellow librarians, empowering them strengthens the awareness of the importance of library programs on the district level, which is particularly important when a new superintendent is hired.

STANDARDS AND ETHICS

Standards have become an integral part of education and librarians have two other elements to include in their practice. Although you have been mindful of Common Core, and now the ramifications of the Every Child Succeeds Act (ESSA) www.ed.gov/essa?src=rn, as a leader, it is even more important that you are solidly grounded in it.

Many years ago when rubrics were introduced into grading student works, a teacher approached me to help her. At that time, I had never constructed a rubric, although I had read enough to understand what they were and how to create one. Together we sat down, and with my input, soon completed one for her upcoming assignment. The teacher never asked me if I had done it before. Based on our many interactions and collaborations she assumed I would know.

Knowing what is in the standards allows you to identify how the library program is an integral part of realizing them. The more you are aware of what the standards contain, the better you are at helping teachers, which makes them value you as an instructional partner and someone they can count on to help them. Just when they had become adjusted to Common Core, they now need to find their way through ESSA and the evolving information about it.

By being among the first to be familiar with ESSA, you will be able to guide teachers and be of support to your administrator who is also struggling to master the new requirements. You don't have to do this alone. AASL has a "landing site" at www.ala.org/aasl/advocacy/legislation/essa, where you can find links to all aspects of ESSA and any updates as new information emerges.

The site is of additional importance to you as ESSA has provisions for the role of school libraries and librarians. These are not automatic. You need to be aware of what they are and how to bring them into your school and district. Your state school library association is also staying on top of this and working with AASL and should have a link on its website. Check in on both sites for the latest information.

National standards for school librarians also need to be incorporated into your lessons and shared with teachers and administrators. ISTE, the International Society for Technology in Education has refreshed their standards for students: www.iste.org/standards/standards/standards-for-students. The six areas of focus include creativity and innovation; communication and collaboration; research and information fluency; critical thinking, problem solving, and decision making; digital citizenship; and technology operations and concepts. All are directly related to learning experiences in the library. Download a copy and keep it handy.

ISTE also has standards for teachers and administrators. These will also be refreshed to reflect the new standards for students. Your administrator may not know these exist, although your tech department probably does. Inform your principal as to how you work with teachers to achieve these standards. It's one more way to show your growing leadership.

The *AASL Standards for the 21st-Century Learner*, www.ala.org/aasl/standards/learning, have been around since 2007. The new standards will out by fall 2017. You need your copy as soon as possible. Once you have it, do not use the old standards. You are a leader and must keep up with changes. You need to be in the forefront. Communicate with the other librarians in your district. Make an effort to have some time during a professional development day to work as a group to integrate the new standards into your lessons.

Just as you need to step up your game around standards now that you are growing stronger as a leader, you also need to be more connected to the ethics of our profession. The core of these is the Code of Ethics of the American Library Association, www.ala.org/advocacy/proethics/codeofethics/codeethics. The eight parts represent the beliefs that shape librarianship,

The material under the first roman numeral is a reminder that we serve *all* our users. It's important to be aware of those you may not be serving as they need, such as children who are homeless (and that might be a reason for an overdue book) or coping with a divorce or loss of a parent, or an extremely challenging home life. The material under the second roman numeral stresses our commitment to intellectual freedom, an often scary place for a solitary school librarian who must make choices that could lead to job termination. As a leader, what do you do?

Another part of the code emphasizes how we protect patron privacy. You need to know the difference between parental rights over their child and what rights the school has in relation to the child's privacy. You also are to recognize the difference between your personal convictions and your professional responsibilities—sometimes translated to mean that every library should contain something that offends someone, including the librarian who ordered it.

And finally, we maintain excellence by continuing to learn and improve our skills. This is particularly true for you as a leader. It has long been true for school librarians that they are responsible for their own professional development. It is even more important for you. Not only do you need to be ahead of the curve, you also should be taking responsibility for ensuring that all the librarians in your district are successful. For the program to truly be valued, all the librarians must be valued.

Although not as central as the ALA Code of Ethics to your professional life, you also must be aware of copyright laws. If you haven't introduced it yet, you should be teaching students how and why to cite as soon as they do any research. Moreover, your students need to learn how to use Creative Commons—and so do your teachers. You can host a workshop for them on a professional development day.

Make sure teachers also understand Fair Use as it applies in education. Many assume as long as they aren't making a profit and it's for educational use, they can use anything and as much of it as they want. There are a number of good resources to use, but you can start with this five-part series from Education World on *The Educator's Guide to Copyright and Fair Use* at www.educationworld .com/a_curr/curr280.shtml.

Being a leader means people are watching you. You want to be an example of someone who operates with integrity. Knowing the ethics that guide our profession and living up to them provide that basis.

STAYING CURRENT

Now more than ever, you must keep up with what's new. As a librarian, you have always done this, from offering the newest books for your students to knowing what tech resources have emerged for sharing, presenting, managing, and organizing information, along with other means of keeping students engaged as they learn and helping teachers. You still need to continue doing this, but as leader you should go further.

Be aware of what is going on in the wider world of education. Tune in to what is happening in technology—not only web resources, but the vast scope of the field. You won't be using quantum computing for some time, but you should know what it is. Down the road this information is likely to have an impact. This way you will not only be ready for it, you will be able to lead the way.

Business and technology are intertwined today. Whether you read a good newspaper or get your information from a digital source, make it a point to find out what is happening in the business world, particularly as it connects to technology. Also look to new approaches businesses are taking. Many of the ideas presented in this book have stemmed from the business world.

Don't overlook the entertainment field. It has ties to both business and technology. Just as important is the role it plays in the life of your students. Where do you put Legos? They were a child's toy for years before they moved into the tech world and then into movies. They have become a common component of Makerspaces, and some of your students play Lego video games.

How do you get all this information without getting swamped? I subscribe to *SmartBriefs on Leadership* and *SmartBriefs on Education*. They are free and come to my e-mail inbox. Sometimes I don't read any of the articles, and rarely more than one. There are other resources to explore as well.

I also have set up a Google Alert on school libraries and another on information literacy. It keeps me abreast of what is happening across the country and worldwide. Finding out about a censorship issue in one place can alert you to a possible challenge in your district. Knowing how it played out helps you prepare for a similar challenge..

For the two Google Alerts I receive, information literacy provides more international information than the school libraries alert. It's interesting to learn where we share common challenges and also discover how people in other countries are working to improve teaching this core skill. The information literacy alert also has more articles from the college level that invariably can be adapted for high school students.

The alerts also carry stories of librarian successes and student projects that received attention in local newspapers. Reading about them may inspire you to try something similar. Sometimes you can even track down the librarian involved to get more information.

In addition to these sources, start reading outside your comfort zone. If your school library is a member of ASCD (Association of Supervision and Curriculum Development) you receive their excellent journal *Educational Leadership*. You also receive a few free books they publish as part of that membership.

Annual membership is not expensive, so consider joining on your own. Each issue of *Educational Leadership* has a theme. Some issues have more connection to your program than others, but each is an indication of trends in education. This is the journal your principal likely reads. By being familiar with the content, you will speak in his or her language and know what the big issues are from an administrative point of view.

Leaders must develop a big-picture approach. As you become more of a presence in your building and district, you want to demonstrate you have a broad perspective that goes beyond what is happening locally. You are able to discuss larger trends confidently. Your expertise is apparent in your conversations, and you and your program are increasingly respected and valued.

SEEK TO INNOVATE

Always have a plan. Chapter 9 discussed the importance of that. Now your plans are bigger and sometimes riskier. Risk is always scary since it carries with it the implication of possible failure. By now you have established your credentials, and while every plan might not work out as you wish or anticipate, the fallout will only be a setback and not cause damage to your reputation.

At the end of the school year, make your own personal scan of your facility and program. Where are they getting old? When was the last time you changed the look of your library? Yes, there are budget issues, but at the moment, you are just assessing, not worrying about how to make it happen.

Are there places in your program you are doing things routinely? Routines suggest you haven't given thought to doing it better. It's not that you are going to change everything. The purpose of the scan is to inspect and evaluate. Could it be done better if it were done differently?

The knowledge base you are building about various trends and successes occurring elsewhere should suggest possible areas where you might want to start planning something new and innovative—something that will make everyone see the library and the library program anew.

Have you ever considered taking your library outside? It's been done. By bringing books to playgrounds and other places kids congregate, you can tie their activities to a collection you bring. You do need to get permission, and you will need a method of checking out material so you keep a record of it.

If you try a project like this, you probably would want to seek a grant to fund it. It could come from a local sporting goods store, or you could seek out any of the online sources such as DonorsChoose.org. By alerting the media—print or cable—you will be able to send your message how libraries build a love of reading and create lifelong learners to a far wider audience than you have had before.

A variation of this is to take your Makerspace program outside. If you have a strong one in place, this might be a novel way to let the community know how the library program helps students with STEM as well as becoming producers of ideas and information. Another example includes a public library that brought a program to a mall. Reading about what is happening in many places will give you ideas for where you want to take your program next.

Changing your library into a learning commons is a major undertaking. A number of places have done so—from elementary through college libraries—and you can tap into their experiences online. A past issue of *Knowledge Quest* discussed this as a theme, so there are numerous quality articles on how and why you should do it...

Pictures abound so you can start envisioning how your learning commons would look. Decide on what your goal is in making this happen. Start working on a strategic plan. Contact those who have successfully done it to see where there are any gaps in your action plan.

Once you know where you want to go with this, approach the key stakeholders who would have to approve the plan. You want to show your principal how the move to a learning commons would bring positive attention to the school. You might also need to get the approval of the superintendent.

By now, you are quite capable of knowing how to reach out to your stakeholders. They have come to respect you and trust your ability to carry a project forward. If you are really daring, prepare a long-range plan to convert all the libraries in the district into learning commons. In the words of Walt Disney, "If you can dream it, you can achieve it."

TOOLKITS

The national organizations offer valuable information for you to implement or adapt on a variety of topics in the form of toolkits. Your state association may have them as well. Check the website to see what is available. AASL has an abundance of them, and you should become familiar with all of them. You never know when one might prove invaluable.

The *Health and Wellness Toolkit*, www.ala.org/aasl/advocacy/tools/toolkits/health-wellness, provides a five-step advocacy program, beginning with "Know Your Stakeholders," including students through legislators. Although you should have your own advocacy plan in place by now, this will help you identify areas you haven't thought of before. You can also use it to work with the other librarians in your district to build a core of advocates for the library program.

If you use the *Health and Wellness Toolkit*, you shouldn't need the *Crisis Toolkit*, www.ala.org/aasl/advocacy/tools/toolkits/crisis, but it's there if a sudden problem arises. This toolkit is meant to be put into action if there is an immediate threat of elimination of librarians and the library. It helps you define the situation, creates a mission statement for the organization, and shares the subsequent steps for how to communicate and craft your message. It also tells you how to connect to get state and national support from AASL and other organizations, and has links to other helpful resources.

You can download a 77-page PDF, *Toolkit for Promoting School Library Programs*, www.ala.org/aasl/advocacy/tools/toolkits/promoting, which you can share with the other librarians in your district. This is a solid introduction to advocacy for those who are somewhat intimidated about undertaking it. The *Parent Advocate Toolkit*, www.ala.org/aasl/advocacy/tools/toolkits/parent-advocate, is a more focused resource. It has ideas for parents to discover why the library program is important and what they can do to ensure their children have one in their school. A link to resources is at the end. The challenge is to get this in the hands of parents. You can refer to it at a back-to-school night, or let the head of your parent-teacher organization know about it.

If you are concerned about dealing with children in foster care, homeless children, children of incarcerated parents, children of migrant workers, and children in nontraditional families, AASL offers *Resource Guide for Undeserved Populations*, www.ala.org/aasl/sites/ala.org.aasl/files/content/aaslissues/toolkits/UnderservedPopulations_toolkit_2016–06–06.pdf. The 60-page PDF has chapters on each of the aforementioned groups of underserved students, with resources, tips, and legislation. Districts struggle with being able to help these children. With this resource in hand, you will be able to institute a plan and help your teachers and administrators.

A much smaller toolkit of sorts is the *Pre-Service Toolkit for Principals and Teachers*, www.ala.org/aasl/sites/ala.org.aasl/files/content/aaslissues/toolkits/PreserviceEducators_Toolkit_FINAL_2016-03-17.pdf. The ten-page PDF created by the Educators of School Librarians Section is meant to prepare teachers and administrators to recognize the resource they have in the school librarian. It is really an extended annotated bibliography of articles, books, brochures, reports, and other resources that document the value of librarians and show how they increase student learning. While it's unlikely you would use it with preservice principals and teachers, you can acquire many items on the bibliography to have on hand and use when working with your principal or a teacher.

ASCD has toolkits but most are not free. They are mainly books for purchase, although they do offer webinars on some topics and have some helpful short PDFs. Search on ASCD Toolkits to see what is available. You might want to acquire some of their books, such as one by Cindy Strickland, *Tools for High-Quality Differentiated Instruction: An ASCD Action Tool*. You and your teachers will likely make use of it.

Keep checking the AASL site for new toolkits. More than the other associations, AASL produces a number of them as issues arise. AASL's Affiliate Assembly, composed of two delegates from state school library associations, brings up the need for one on a topic and charges the AASL Board to see that it's done. The result is a new toolkit.

Stay aware of these and other resources so you can keep your program fresh and moving forward. Use the many resources available to you to help your fellow librarians in the district to also make needed changes. For your ultimate success, all the librarians need to be successful as well.

KEY IDEAS

- » When you empower someone, you help them feel more confident and sure of their abilities.
- » Leaders need to empower their stakeholders.
- » Through your teaching, readers' advisory, and one-on-one help, you empower students.
- » You empower teachers by helping them with technology and current educational practices.
- » Keeping administrators aware of the tech resources being integrated into instruction, and showcasing the work of teachers whose classes have used the library, empower administrators.
- » Providing resources on cyber safety, and informing parents of class work involving their children, empower parents.
- » Empower volunteers by trusting them to complete tasks, balancing inspiring with inspecting.

» All the librarians in the district are empowered by sharing what projects and activities are occurring in the different school libraries.
» You empower team members by giving them individual credit for their responsibility in completing specific parts of the committee's work.
» Keep monitoring the AASL and your state association's website to stay current with ESSA so you can help teachers and the other librarians in your district.
» Download a copy of the new ISTE standards for students and integrate them into your teaching.
» Do the same with the new iteration of AASL standards and see how to move from the 2007 standards to the new ones in your lessons.
» Learn and live up to the ALA Code of Ethics.
» Know the copyright laws, including Fair Use, as they apply in education, and teach students and teachers about them.
» Become more aware of what is going on in the larger world of education, technology, business, and entertainment to be prepared for trends that may impact school library programs in your district.
» Use resources, such as newspapers, online sources, and Google Alerts to stay informed about these areas.
» Assess your facility and your program for what has become old or routine and consider what innovative changes you can make.
» Use the resources you have been reading to help decide what to do, such as taking your library outside or turning it into a learning commons.
» Once you know what you want to do, make a strategic plan to accomplish it and check with those who have done something similar to see if you have any gaps in your action plan.
» Consider how you can stretch even more to have everyone see your library and program anew.
» Become familiar with the toolkits offered by national associations and any offered by your state.
» Share toolkits, particularly those as PDFs, with other librarians in your district so you can work together to make significant improvements to district-wide library programs.

Notes

1. Carroll, Lewis. *Through the Looking Glass and What Alice Found There*. 32–33. https://birrell.org/andrew/alice/lGlass.pdf.
2. Merriam Webster. "Empower." www.merriam-webster.com/dictionary/empower.

CHAPTER ELEVEN

MAINTAINING JOY

We are approaching the end of this journey into leadership, but it's really one without an end. I always love the quote by Ursula LeGuin, from the *Left Hand of Darkness*: "It's good to have an end to journey towards; but it's the journey that matters in the end." You will always have an end in mind, but when you get there, in the distance you will see another milestone you want to reach. And so you continue to grow until it seems you have always been a leader, and you cannot remember why you thought it would be difficult to become one.

At this point in your growth, it's time you thought of leading on a higher stage. At the same time, you must take care that you aren't only focusing on doing. In the words of the old adage, "all work and no play, makes Jack a dull boy," it's a phrase we have forgotten in our 24/7 world. If all you do is give, you will wake up one morning and find there is nothing left. You are drained and exhausted.

In this final chapter of the book, we will look at how to live a balanced life. Yes, you will expand your leadership roles and capabilities, but not at the expense of having joy in your life. When you can lead and still make time for the people and things you love, you inspire others to risk the road to leadership.

WRITING AND PRESENTING

Few librarians give any thought to writing, yet it's an excellent place to take your leadership. Sharing what you have learned to help others puts you in the role of a mentor, whether readers seek you out further or not. It also requires the self-confidence you have built and the willingness to take risks.

Any traces of the imposter syndrome in you will show up as you contemplate writing. It's a case of "who am I to tell someone else what to do?" If it's something you learned from your experience, you are likely to feel it is presumptuous on your part when you haven't done a research study to prove it is accurate.

The feeling of risk comes from knowing once something is out there in print, it's open to criticism. You will never get unanimous approval. Hearing and reading negative comments about something you worked hard on to produce are painful. You will need to recognize that other than official reviews, you always hear much more from those with a negative view.

That said, if you are willing to take on the challenge of writing, where do you begin? You can accustom yourself to writing by starting a blog. Have a schedule for how frequently you will write new posts. This will hold you accountable to yourself. The length of the post is up to you. Some bloggers have a single theme, such as what they are doing with their students, but yours can be as varied as you like. If you post regularly, you can discuss books in your collection one week, and a webinar or presentation that taught you something another week. The idea is to share information and become comfortable with writing.

For a somewhat more daring venture—into print publishing—think of writing an article. It could be for your state association's newsletter if you want to start small and in a safe environment. See if you can do a regular column on a subject of interest to you that might be helpful to others. Advocacy building is a possibility.

The national library associations publish journals and if you write to the editor you can find out their themes for the year. If one resonates with you, offer to write an article. For example, *Knowledge Quest*, AASL's journal, wants articles to be 2,500 words or less. *Knowledge Quest* also has an online blog and looks for librarians who will make regular posts. Check out their website and think of what you might contribute.

Once you have your feet wet as a writer, you can think about writing a book. It's not as hard as you would imagine. Create an outline of what you would include in the book. This becomes your draft table of contents.

Make a list of the publishers who have issued books you have purchased. At a conference, speak to them. There are a number of possibilities, including ALA Editions. Pitch your idea and see if you get any takers. If you have some writing credits, such as an article in a magazine or a known blog, you increase your chances of editors and publishers taking interest..

Chapter 8 suggested you begin making presentations by starting with a department or grade-level meeting. The purpose is to help you get past any fears about speaking before groups, accustom you to making a presentation for adults, and to demonstrate your expertise and leadership. The next step is to submit a program for your state association's conference.

In many districts, you might have difficulty getting professional time to attend a conference, but it tends to be easier if your administration knows you will be presenting. Being selected by the conference program committee indicates they recognize the value of your expertise, and shows your administrators you are seen as someone who has something worthwhile to contribute.

If you have created a strong inquiry-based unit with a teacher, consider doing the presentation jointly. This serves a number of purposes: You won't be up there in the front of the room on your own, you will be promoting the excellence of a colleague, and, once again, this will show your administrators how you contribute to the school program as well as bring it prestige.

With the experience of a state conference to bolster your confidence, it's time to attempt a national conference. It's far more difficult to get your proposal accepted at this level, and to make the prospect easier for you and more likely that your idea will be approved, try for a poster session. This gets you a national audience, but for the most part, you are speaking to people one-on-one.

Your leadership skills will improve as a result, your confidence will grow, and you will have definitely moved out of your old comfort zone. It is a powerful ego boost to see how many fellow librarians are interested in the project you are showcasing and to have them ask you questions about it. National leaders are usually present, and they will notice what you are doing. Meeting the people you have heard about or read articles by in the journals makes you realize you are one of them. Someday it could—and should—be you who is seen as a national leader.

As you might expect, the next step is to do a presentation at a national conference. By this time, you have become accustomed to speaking in front of large groups of adults. You have confidence in your knowledge and trust in your abilities to present a worthwhile program. More and more, you see yourself as leader.

DELEGATING

For most librarians, one of the most challenging leadership skills is the ability to delegate. The reality is that the more you take on, the larger the stage you play on, the greater the necessity you have to delegate—for several reasons. The most obvious is that you cannot get everything done on your own.

At various times, you may need people with talents and abilities different from yours. On a very simple level, I recognize I am a big-picture person, which means I can miss important details that need to get done. I always look to enroll people who are very detail oriented, and I make sure they know to alert me to something I may have overlooked, even if it seems obvious to them.

One small example is when I was involved in directing a three-year renovation of my high school library. We couldn't expand the walls, so we went to movable shelves for about 90 percent of the collection, with counter-height shelving below and in front of the large wall of windows. I planned on using those shelves for fiction books. My detail-oriented co-librarian pointed out that putting heavy reference books (we used many more then) on tall shelves was a bad idea. I agreed, and we put the reference collection there instead.

If you are always doing things alone, people come to assume you are some type of super person and they never offer to help. Remember, you are in the relationship business. You don't always want to be giving. People need and want an opportunity to give back, to feel they are making a contribution, and are valued.

What is the difficulty in delegating? Primarily, it means you have to give up some control. Most likely, the task will not be accomplished the way you would have done it. It may not be as perfect as you would like. Accept that. In the larger scheme of things, it is rarely that important. It is important to take the job off your plate (although not completely) and give someone else an opportunity to learn and grow from doing it.

It's important to note that the job is not completely off your plate because when you take on a project, it is your responsibility to see that it is done in a satisfactory manner. It doesn't mean you have to do the work, but you are responsible for the end product. So how do you balance delegating and being accountable for the result?

This is where you demonstrate your leadership. As explained in Chapter 10, when leading a team, you inspire and inspect. When you assign a task to someone, make sure they understand what is wanted and have an opportunity to safely ask questions to clarify what is expected. Tell them by when you would like the job completed. Let them know they can come to you if they run into any problems or see that they will need more time.

Allow people to figure out their own method for completing a task. They need to find an approach that works with who they are. Every so often check in with them. Use the time to cheer them on, asking them to share with you what they are finding out.

You don't want to come off as not trusting them, but in the course of the conversation you might see that it will take longer than expected to complete their piece. Ask if they would like more time and if there is anything else they need. If you do this well, they will feel confident in their ability to succeed and feel safe in asking you for help if necessary.

Selecting someone to take on a task is another challenge of delegating. You may find it uncomfortable to ask for help. There is always the chance the person will say "no," and that might affect your future relationship. Your relationships, however, are the key. If you have built strong ones, you have primary "go-to" people for help. It could be a volunteer, paraprofessional, a teacher, or possibly a student.

You should know the person well enough to be confident they can do the job. Most people tend not to refuse requests,, so don't set them up for failure. Don't ask in a hesitant way. Saying something like, "I really need help in doing (insert the task), and I thought of you immediately. I know you can handle it, and it would mean so much to me if you were the one to take it on." Be ready to explain when the job needs to be completed, and assure the person you will be there to answer any questions.

Delegating is another form of risk taking. You give up some control and risk the project not being completed to your specific expectations, and yet you are responsible for the outcome. You need to credit success to the participants for their contributions and accept responsibility for any failures. It's why so many librarians avoid it. Leaders must embrace it.

Dress for Success

You know by now that you communicate a great deal without words. Body language tells a lot about what you are thinking and how you are feeling. How you dress also sends messages.

Look around your building. Note how the teachers dress. Is there a difference between those who are well regarded and others? The dress of the secretarial and clerical staff is rarely the same as teachers. Paraprofessionals and aides often have their own similar dress code, although this is not a hard and fast rule. There are always exceptions, but in general this holds true.

Now look at how administrators dress. Compare that with what you wear. Where are you on the scale? If you look like some of the less-regarded teachers, you are opening yourself up to being ignored or not valued highly. If your clothes are similar to teachers who are highly regarded, you are in a better position.

But you want more than that. You want to be viewed as a leader. Increasingly, you will be in the presence of administrators. If you look more like you are one of them, you will be treated as though you are. It may seem shallow, but it's effective.

I have known a few librarian leaders and one administrator who didn't "dress for success," but they are rarities. They are incredibly skilled at showing their worth and so were accepted by everyone for the leaders they are. You, on the other hand, are still at a place where you want to prove yourself and emerge from how you are currently perceived.

Dressing for success is much discussed in the business world but hardly ever mentioned in education. Indeed, in some corporations, a person who is being primed for promotion to higher levels of management might be sent to a personal shopper to be able to present a more polished, successful appearance. Unlike the corporate world, in a school system, upgrading your wardrobe doesn't mean you will be purchasing clothes with designer labels, but being mindful of the message you send with what you are wearing is important.

A reality check is necessary here. If you are at the elementary school level, skirts and dresses for women and suits for men are impractical. You frequently get down on the floor to work with kids. However, nice pant suits or their equivalent, and ties and such for men are a subtle change that will be taken in subliminally as part of your message.

While you are unlikely to work on the floor with students in high school, the same suggestions can hold. Most important at any level is to feel comfortable with what you wear. Flashy jewelry and long, dangling earrings should generally be avoided as they are distracting.

Shoes are another consideration. High heels for women are impractical unless you are very accustomed to moving in them. Sneakers, on the other hand, need to be carefully thought out. Some are very casual, while others might work, depending on the norms in your building and district. Although it's not fair, men more easily get away with them.

In becoming a leader, it pays to be mindful of things big and small. You show your leadership in what you do and who you are, and that is what is most important. But you don't want the small things to take away or diminish in any way from how you are perceived.

GIVING BACK

In becoming a leader, you were helped along the way. A librarian mentored you or just gave you some good advice. Your state and national organization provided resources from which you drew. No one emerges as a full-blown leader all on their own—not even if they are natural-born leaders.

Now that you have demonstrated your leadership abilities, are being taken seriously, and your program is regarded as vital to both student and teacher success, it is time to give back. In Chapter 5 you were encouraged to seek out a mentor. Now it's time to become one.

Becoming a Mentor

Once you accept your responsibility to become a mentor, you need to find mentees. One of the most important things you can do as a leader in your district is to ensure that all the librarians are successful and seen as leaders. Check to see if your district has any new hires. Positions that once were eliminated are slowly (OK, very slowly) being restored in certain parts of the country. Today—unlike years in the recent past—when a librarian leaves or retires, that position is not eliminated, so districts are getting more new librarians. Reach out to these newbies and offer your services.

You can also mentor at the state level. If your state association doesn't have a mentorship program, propose one. If you are not a member of the board, go on you state association's discussion board and suggest a core of volunteer mentors for new librarians, saying you would want to be one and help those starting out be successful.

The simple act of putting yourself out there should bring requests from those who recognize what a gift this is as well as volunteers who will join you in becoming mentors. Use a national forum, such as LM_NET or AASL_Forum to find out which states have a program and are willing to share it with you. (No need to re-create the wheel.)

Once you have reached out and some, or even one, librarians are interested, make sure they understand the nature of this relationship. Both mentors and mentees have responsibilities in this relationship and it's best if these are discussed clearly from the beginning. The mentee has the obligation of honoring the mentor's time and using the communication channel the mentor prefers—whether it's phone, e-mail, skype, or whatever seems best; sometimes the mentor can come to the mentee's library. Also determine the frequency of communications. It can be on an as-needed basis, or there can be a regular schedule.

Additionally, the mentee must be clear as to his or her needs. What specifically does the mentee want to know or learn? I have had mentees e-mail me a copy of an evaluation they received, explained what happened, and asked for the best way to respond to it. I have been asked to help craft a memo to a principal regarding a problem situation and do it in a way that the librarian didn't sound as though she was whining or complaining.

It is also a good idea for the mentee to keep track of the number and content of the communications. This serves as documentation of the mentee's growth. If kept general enough, the mentee might be able to use it to show the principal what he/she learned.

The role of the mentor is more than simply that of a coach. The mentor cheers on the mentee on those down days when all seems to be going wrong and points to places where the mentee has shown growth. Mentors need to be good listeners and not rush in with answers and advice. They should ask guiding questions, much the way we do with students. It's important that the mentees learn to think through problems and situations on their own.

The mentor is also the mentee's link to resources. This includes reminding them of national association websites, informing them of tech resources and apps, as well as connecting and introducing them to other leaders. Slowly, the mentor guides the mentee not only to be confident and successful on the job, but more importantly, the mentor helps the mentee on the path to leadership.

Serving on a Larger Stage

You probably have served on or even chaired a committee in your school and district. Perhaps you have done the same for your state association. All of these are excellent paths in leadership, but there is more to do in giving back. First look for ways to serve on your state association's board of directors. Let the president know if you wish to chair a standing committee, which will put you on the board.

Once there, plan on running for office. There is no better way to give back than by volunteering to serve in a library association whose mission is to help librarians and promote the value of library programs. As a member of the board, you become aware of the state level political situations that affect librarians at the building level. You will see the scope of challenges librarians are facing and become part of the campaign to make changes.

While waiting for a spot to open up, volunteer to serve on a national committee. Working at that level might seem intimidating at first, but you will find everyone is welcoming and eager to help you settle in. Working on the national level is eye-opening. You discover where challenges are similar across the country and what situations are developing that you haven't seen in your state but are now prepared to handle, should they arise.

One of the unexpected benefits of serving at the state, and even more so on the national level, is what occurs to your vocabulary. You develop a fluency in talking about the value of school librarians and what a strong library program brings to students, teachers, and the educational committee as a whole. In talking with administrators and others, you sound like the expert you have become, and you are taken much more seriously.

Some of you might have reservations about volunteering at this level because of the time and financial requirements. ALA has two meetings a year, Annual and Midwinter. ISTE and AECT have one. Their locations vary from year to year, but inevitably require travel and sometimes days off from your job.

ALA does permit you to be a virtual member, which means you don't have to attend in person. Much committee work these days is conducted on conference calls to complete major tasks before conferences. Still volunteering is a commitment. You take it on when you recognize the importance of giving back. You also understand it is important to you as a leader and the leader you are yet to be to serve on a larger level.

If at all possible, do attend these national conferences. The sheer size is overwhelming at first. There are many programs to consider seeing, and the exhibits will fill you with ideas. I have never met anyone who didn't go home exhilarated and motivated by what they saw and heard. You make connections with other leaders, sometimes those at the very top, and they become part of your growing PLN. Once you go, you are likely to become like most of us who look forward each time to these meetings.

Two quotes to keep in mind: The first is anonymous, "If serving is beneath you, leadership is beyond you." While you might not consider serving beneath you, failing to serve will keep you from true leadership.

The second quote is attributed to Elizabeth Warren, and I have seen variations of it: "If you don't have a seat at the table, you are probably on the menu." Scary and, unfortunately, accurate. As a leader, you are in the best position to ensure librarians have a seat at the table.

THE GIFT OF TIME

It's been a long journey since you first took on the challenge of becoming a leader. You have analyzed yourself, stepped out of your comfort zone, and are now demonstrating leadership. The journey, of course, never ends, but books do and this one is drawing to a close.

What is left is not about leadership directly. It's about life. Time is a gift and a finite commodity. You were concerned about having the time to be a leader. Now you must recognize the wisdom of not investing all your time and energy in being one.

If you are to survive and thrive as a leader you need to live a balanced life. You can never get back moments you didn't share with family and friends because you were too busy. What are your priorities? Too many people, and I was once that way, would answer, "family," but their actions and choices show otherwise.

Yes, there are times when you need to stay late. Once in a while you may go into work on a Saturday. But if you are coming home late every night, you are cheating those you care most about and yourself. You have developed your EI to be aware of what is going on under your colleagues' exteriors, but are you doing the same with your significant other, good friends, and whoever else is important in your life?

When you are home, be fully present. Let school slip away from your consciousness. Don't spend your time thinking about the job and your next project. Focus on the people around you. Make time to have lunch or dinner with friends.

Living a balanced life is also a gift to other librarians who are watching you. As a leader, you are a role model. You exemplify what leadership entails. If all you are is a workaholic, reasonable people will not see the value in emulating you, and you do want to build more leaders. Tom Peters has said, "Leaders don't create followers, they create more leaders," (www.brainyquote.com/quotes/quotes/t/tompeters382508.html).

It's wise to remember you are a human *being*, not a human *doing*. Don't let work be your life. Live your life fully. Laugh, play, work—and lead.

KEY IDEAS

» Expand your leadership skills by writing articles for your state newsletter, blog posts for national newsletters, such as *Knowledge Quest*, and for national association journals.

» With some writing credit in your background, consider writing a book for fellow librarians.

» At conferences, pitch your idea to publishers of books for librarians.

» Write a proposal to do a presentation at your next state conference.

» Consider doing a presentation in conjunction with a teacher with whom you have created a successful project.

» Move on to the national scene by submitting a proposal for a poster session at a national conference.

» With your new-found confidence at addressing your colleagues, you are ready to submit a proposal for a national conference.

» Delegating is challenging because it requires you to give up control.

» When you assign a part of a project to someone, don't tell them how to do it, trust they will get it done. But inspect every so often to be sure no problems are being encountered.

» Delegating gives other people an opportunity to feel they contribute and are valued.

» Compare your dress to that of other teachers and administrators to see those you most emulate.

» Alter your wardrobe to be more like that of leaders, such as administrators, to have people view you that way.

» Now that you are more established as a leader it's time to give back and help others as you were helped.

» Become a mentor to new librarians in your district, by seeking out or creating a mentorship program with your state library association.

» Recognize the different responsibilities of mentors and mentees.

» Volunteer to serve on a standing committee of your state association, and
  plan to run for office.
» Volunteer to serve on a national level committee. It is a stretch but you
  reap many rewards.
» Do your best to attend a national conference.
» Live a balanced life. Never neglect family and friends for work.

INDEX